KU-753-964

CONTENTS

SYMBOLS & ABBREVIATIONS

The following symbols are used throughout this book:

@ address **t** telephone **f** fax **e** email **w** website address
○ opening times **Ⓝ** public transport connections **!** important

The following symbols are used on the maps:

i	information office	○	city
✈	airport	○	large town
✚	hospital	○	small town
👮	police station	=	motorway
🚌	bus station	—	main road
✝	cathedral	—	minor road
❶	numbers denote featured cafés & restaurants		

Hotels and restaurants are graded by approximate price as follows:
£ budget **££** mid-range **£££** expensive

▶ *Striking modern architecture in Dubai's financial district*

Introduction

Dubai glitteringly defies most, if not all, traditional notions of desert lifestyles. In this fast-paced, architecturally stunning city the average sheikh feeds petrol to his Ferrari instead of water to his camel and buys his body-covering *dishdasha* from an air-conditioned mall instead of a souk.

Set between Europe and Asia, Dubai is the jewel in the crown of the United Arab Emirates (UAE). It is the second largest of the seven Emirates (Abu Dhabi, Ajman, Fujaira, Ras al-Khaimah, Sharjah and Umm al-Qaiwain being the other six) and is located on the southern shore of the Arabian Gulf.

Visitors who arrive in Dubai expecting a hot, dusty, barren town surrounded by hostile desert find instead a clean, dynamic and – in some parts – lush green city, straddling a natural harbour flanked by sparkling Gulf waters and attractive sandy beaches. The hinterland is largely desert and arid mountains, but it is tamed just enough by the tour guides to enable urban adventurers to roam its dunes and wadis for a glimpse of the last frontier.

The city appears to have evolved almost overnight, with new hotels and shopping centres constantly springing up like mushrooms. A series of man-made islands in the shapes of palm trees and the globe, so large they are visible from outer space, have also been built to create even more land for building.

For a glimpse of Old Dubai, while it still exists, head to the old Bastakiya district. The narrow streets here will remind you of days gone by, and the old wind towers, which helped cool desert houses before the advent of electricity and air conditioning, are the mark of Dubai. This district is now being restored to show tourists the true old city, far from the glass and steel skyscrapers that now define the area.

But those too have exerted a fascination: Dubai is a true look at Arabia of the past, present and future.

◆ *Tradition meets towers on Dubai Creek*

When to go

You are never likely to experience bad weather in Dubai, which is what makes it such a popular year-round destination. The average temperature in January is 18°C (65°F); in July it is a rather more uncomfortable 33°C (92°F). The average annual rainfall is 15¼ cm (6 in). Between October and April is the best time to visit, when the sun shines more benignly and temperatures are between 20°C (68°F) and 30°C (86°F). This is understandably prime time for tourists, so hotels definitely require advance reservations. Don't expect any bargain-basement pricing. The season reaches an all-time peak with the Dubai Shopping Festival taking place from mid-January to mid-February. If you don't find soaring temperatures and high humidity a drawback, however, book your holiday for the month of September, when hotels offer dramatic rate reductions to lure tourists.

There is another important element to keep in mind when planning your journey to Dubai aside from the excessive heat of the summer months, when temperatures can soar uncomfortably high, and that's the holy month of Ramadan (see page 15). During Ramadan, when Muslims fast from dawn to dusk, the entire city is affected. In the daytime many restaurants refuse to serve alcohol, food or even water. Everyone, regardless of their religious persuasion, is obliged to abide by the fast in public. Also, you won't be able to smoke in public, as this is another taboo during this religious observance. So, if your visit should coincide with Ramadan, be prepared for the impact on day-to-day city life. Hardest hit is Dubai's nightlife. Most bars won't even open until about seven in

● *Tropical delight at Jumeirah Beach*

CITYSPOTS
DUBAI

Zoë Ross

Written by Zoë Ross
Original photography by Christopher Holt
Front cover photography © Izzet Keribar/Lonely Planet Images
Series design based on an original concept by Studio 183 Limited

Produced by Cambridge Publishing Management Ltd
Project Editor: Penny Isaac
Layout: Julie Crane
Maps: PC Graphics

Published by Thomas Cook Publishing
A division of Thomas Cook Tour Operations Limited
Company Registration No. 1450464 England
PO Box 227, Unit 18, Coningsby Road
Peterborough PE3 8SB, United Kingdom
email: books@thomascook.com
www.thomascookpublishing.com
+44 (0)1733 416477

ISBN-13: 978-184157-622-0
ISBN-10: 1-84157-622-0

First edition © 2006 Thomas Cook Publishing
Text © 2006 Thomas Cook Publishing
Maps © 2006 Thomas Cook Publishing
Series/Project Editor: Kelly Anne Pipes
Production/DTP: Steven Collins

Printed and bound in Spain by GraphyCems

the evening and, in deference to a ban on live music, the stages remain silent.

ANNUAL EVENTS

January

Dubai Shopping Festival A pull-out-all-the-stops month-long extravaganza that draws shopaholics from around the globe. Shops and malls offer spectacular discounts, and the city revels in displays of fireworks and outdoor festivities. ⓦ www.mydsf.com

Dubai International Jazz Festival This music festival coincides with the shopping festival and features a wide range of performers from many genres. ⓦ www.dubaijazzfest.com

February

Dubai Tennis Open Attracts top players of the international circuit. Events from both the World Tennis Association and the Association of Tennis Professionals provide a full fortnight of activities. ⓦ www.dubaitennischampionships.com

March

Dubai World Cup Held on the last Saturday in March, both genuine horse-racing enthusiasts and celebrities are drawn here to see who will scoop the $15 million prize money. ⓦ www.dubaiworldcup.com

Dubai Desert Classic Entices top golfers to partake in this high-stakes golf match. Expect to see many golfing stars. ⓦ www.dubaidesertclassic.com

June
Dubai Summer Surprises Bargain shopping with hotel prices to match. This summer sale-athon is intended to fill a slow summer season. ⓦ www.mydsf.com

September
Dhow Racing Begins in September and runs until May, with traditional dhow sailing races occurring on a regular basis. Crewed by up to 100 oarsmen and the wind, these ships are a spectacle in motion. ⓦ www.dimc-uae.com

October
UAE Desert Challenge The world's best rally and motor-cross drivers assemble for a high-octane race in the desert. Car, truck and motorcycle categories make this the biggest motorsports event in the UAE. ⓦ www.uaedesertchallenge.com

PUBLIC HOLIDAYS

New Year's Day 1 January

Great British Day 15 January

Prophet Mohammed's Birthday 21 April

Accession Day of His Highness Sheikh Zayed 6 August

UAE National Day 2 December

UIM Class One World Offshore Powerboat Championships More
engines. More money. This time the race takes place on water.
Monster crowds gather to watch these high-powered vessels slice
through the water. ⓦ www.dimc-uae.com

December
National Day (2 December) A three-day holiday celebrating the
founding of the UAE in 1971. The days are filled with an abundance
of cultural events at many venues.

Dubai Rugby Sevens What do you get when you combine sun,
beer and 250 rugby games? One great party in the desert! Held
over three days, matches begin as early as 08.00 and continue
late into the night, as does the activity at the bars and clubs.
ⓦ www.dubairugby7s.com

◀ *Watch the desert driving challenge*

Islamic holidays

Islamic holidays are based on the Islamic calendar. There are
12 months in the Islamic Hijra calendar: Muharram, Safar, Rabi' al-
Awwal, Rabi' al-Akhir, Jumada' al-Ula, Jumada' al-Akhirah, Rajab,
Sha'baan, Ramadan, Shawwal, Dhul-Qi'dah and Dhul-Hijjah. Each
month is 29 or 30 days long, making the Hijra year shorter than the
Western Gregorian year. Unlike the Gregorian day, which is from
midnight to midnight, the Muslim day starts and ends at sunset.
The Hijra calendar began with Prophet Mohammed's migration
from Mecca to Medina. The first year corresponds to AD 622 in the
Gregorian calendar.

It is important to understand that Islamic dates are not fixed:
rather they depend on the sighting of the new moon each month.
For example, the celebratory Eid al-Fitr is often only fixed the
evening before, so everyone must watch the evening news or read
the morning paper for information. This can be a source of anxiety
for newcomers, who can suddenly find that travel plans or other
activities need to be cancelled at very short notice.

Holidays subject to change according to the sighting of the
moon are:

Hijra New Year (January in 2006 & 2007)

Lailat al-Mi'raj: the Prophet's miraculous night journey to Heaven
(August in 2006 & 2007)

Ramadan: month-long fast (starts September in 2006 & 2007)

Eid al-Fitr: Feast of Fast-breaking at the end of Ramadan
(October in 2006 & 2007)

Eid al-Adha: Feast of Sacrifice; occurs during the pilgrimage to
Mecca, commemorating the example set by Prophet Abraham
(January in 2006, December in 2006 & 2007)

RAMADAN

Ramadan, one of the major observances of the Islamic religion, changes almost all aspects of daily life for 30 days every year. During that time, followers devote themselves fully to the tenets of Islam and this unique period of sacrifice. During Ramadan, eating, drinking and smoking are not allowed from sunrise to sunset.

During the day, most businesses reduce their schedules, opening only for around six hours, largely to combat the tiredness and weakness felt by those fasting over such a period of time. Things that would normally be efficiently achieved will generally take a lot longer during Ramadan. Hotel restaurants will stay open to accommodate visitors, but other eating places will close, and it is considered very bad form to eat, drink or smoke openly during Ramadan, even if you are a non-Muslim. Ramadan is a very important aspect of the Islamic calendar and lifestyle, and as a visitor it falls on you to respect the traditions and culture and to exercise patience.

However, when the sun has set, life resumes in a joyful – if not frantic – fashion. Following evening prayers, families and friends gather together for meals, and the streets and shopping malls buzz with the convivial relief of being fed and watered. Even the television networks take part, with special programmes or presentations running later into the evening than is usual.

At the conclusion of this month-long observance comes Eid al-Fitr, a three-day celebration of family and feasting. Following morning prayers, families spend the days together welcoming family and friends with snacks and sweets.

History

The history of Dubai is a peaceful one, based largely on the development of trade and prudent investment rather than warfare.

There is evidence of settlements as far back as the end of the Ice Age, and evidence of trade starting around 5000 BC. The first permanent settlement started around 2500 BC, which made its money from the agriculture of date palms and trade in copper from nearby mines. However, this settlement seems to have disappeared round 2000 BC.

Development started again around AD 700 when Muslim nomads settled in the area to take advantage of the emerging trade routes between the Mediterranean Sea and the Indian Ocean. A port developed, and when Marco Polo passed through in 1580, he described Dubai as a prosperous town.

European traders arrived in the 1600s and drove the Muslim traders away. Somehow Dubai survived by developing a fishing and pearling industry. By 1800, Britannia was ruling the waves, including those in the Gulf. The British navy cleared the area of pirates, and started making deals with local sheikhs to ensure the safety of the British trade routes to India.

Modern history began in 1833, when the Bani Yas tribe moved from Abu Dhabi to Dubai and, with British help, established an independent city. The leader of the tribe was Maktoum Bin Butti, and the Maktoum family continues to rule Dubai to this day.

The Maktoum family maintained good relations with the British, and Dubai started to grow, mainly due to pearling, but with trade increasing. Treaties in the 1870s made Dubai the main British port in the Gulf, and the city expanded even further. In 1894, Sheikh Maktoum Bin Hasker declared Dubai a free port, with tax exemptions for foreign traders. This move, coupled with political problems in Iran, made Dubai the most important port in the Gulf, and the city flourished.

In 1930, the pearling industry collapsed due to the Depression and to the development of cultured pearls in Japan. Dubai responded by allowing for re-export from the port, and trade increased even more. World War II also helped secure Dubai's importance, due to its strategic location.

After World War II, Dubai borrowed heavily to improve and expand its port facilities. Trade again increased, and the new-found wealth was used to modernise and improve the infrastructure of the city.

In 1966, oil was discovered in Dubai, and during the 1970s and 1980s the oil wealth was used to expand the port and to build Dubai into a fully modern, world-class city.

After being the controlling and protective force in the Gulf for 150 years, the British withdrew in 1971, but not before helping the sheikhdoms in the area form the United Arab Emirates (UAE), with Dubai as its second-largest state. The UAE has continued to maintain peace in the area.

Today, the oil is running out and makes up only 10 per cent of Dubai's revenue. However, trade continues to bring prosperity, and tourism is emerging as a new source of income.

Lifestyle

If a single word could convey the essence of the lifestyle in Dubai, it would be tolerance. Foreigners are free to practise their own religion, drink alcohol (in designated locations) and to dress as they would at home, provided that reasonable discretion is shown. Remember, a bathing suit is appropriate on the beach or by the pool but not in town.

Because Dubai's culture is firmly rooted in the traditions of Islam and Arabia, you will find the people to be warm and hospitable. Despite its rapid transition into a 21st-century world, Dubai remains close to its traditions. Local citizens dress in traditional robes called *kandoura* or *dishdasha*, men add a cap called a *gahfia*, and many women will cover their faces with a veil.

As Dubai society is respectful of foreign religious traditions, so it expects that foreigners will respect the traditions of Islam. Ramadan is the major religious holiday, which lasts for almost a month. During this 30-day period Muslims do not eat, drink or smoke during the day, and only the very young or infirm are exempt from this practice. Foreigners are also expected not to eat, drink or smoke during the day in public places as a sign of respect (see page 15).

Family remains at the heart of the society. This is a country where marriages are arranged, families are large and women are respected. Many women in Dubai now work outside the home and they are allowed to drive vehicles and walk unescorted.

City life is a melting pot of many cultures, and although each individual or community strives to assert its unique qualities,

● *Enjoy outdoor dining at any time of year*

they are all seemingly united in civic pride. Dubai can be a very pleasant place to work and live. It features all the modern conveniences of an affluent Western city, with reliable electricity, adequate water, communications that are state of the art, modern hospitals, sporting facilities and, of course, cheap petrol. For this reason, the city has an extremely large expatriate community. In addition there is an absence of the problems common to many modern cities these days – here there is no air pollution, no traffic jams, no poverty and very little crime.

Trade is the main activity of Dubai's business heart, as it has been for many generations. The city is known in the Middle East as the 'city of merchants'. However, tourism, service and construction are rapidly expanding enterprises helping to create a balanced and diverse economy.

Social hours are Mediterranean in style, with the local folk starting work early, frequently taking a long midday break, and then working late into the evening. Thursdays and Fridays comprise the 'weekend', so if you are visiting during a Saturday and Sunday, expect to find all sorts of businesses up and running, including government agencies.

Nightlife is a major feature of the Dubai lifestyle. Hotels have bars and pubs. There are discotheques and lots of foreign-cuisine eateries. Don't expect to find alcohol served outside of hotels, however – permission to drink alcohol is a privilege reserved primarily for foreigners.

Don't think the inhabitants of Dubai are living too abundantly with their dwindling oil supply, though. They were smart enough to plan ahead economically to soften the blow, and tourism is one of their main plans. Dubai is able to boast an Arabian experience in a protected, open-minded city.

One peculiarity of Dubai life, which is unlikely to be apparent to any visitor, is 'wusta'. The concept of having 'wusta' means to have influence in society. If you have been born into the right circles, which in the Emirates translates into the right tribe, you have *wusta* and can get things done – be it a government contract or a table at the best restaurant. Those who have *wusta* tend to take it for granted; the remainder wishes for it in vain.

⬤ *Trade is at the heart of Dubai's economy*

● *Dubai boasts a rich mix of cultures*

WOMEN TRAVELLERS IN THE UAE

Don't let stereotypes or misunderstandings dissuade you from travelling to Dubai and other areas of the UAE if you're female. The rules here are different, but not so extreme as to keep you from visiting. Follow a few simple tips and your experience in the Emirates can only be enhanced.

Incidentally, it's perfectly acceptable for a woman to go straight to the front of a queue or to ask to be served first before any men that may be waiting. This practice is intended to keep you safe from the prying eyes of men and to remove temptation from those who would gaze upon you.

THE RULES FOR WOMEN: DOS & DON'TS

DO ...

- Dress modestly. Avoid shorts, t-shirts and sleeveless attire. The more skin you expose the more attention, sometimes unwanted, you will attract. Dressing modestly means covering arms, legs, shoulders and neckline. But don't despair – baggy shirts and long skirts will not only keep you cooler in the desert heat, they will also protect you from the sun.
- When possible, ask a woman for directions or assistance rather than a man.
- While travelling on public transport, try to sit next to other women.
- Avoid direct eye contact with local men. Wearing sunglasses is a great help.
- Wear a ring on your wedding finger. It gives the appearance that you are not available.
- Be observant in crowds or other places where people are packed tightly together – crude things have been known to occur.
- When dining alone, ask to be seated in the family section if one is available.
- Having trouble shaking off an 'admirer'? Head for the nearest hotel lobby, bank or shop. If you need help, ask someone to telephone the police.

DON'T ...

- respond to vulgar or rude comments.
- sit in the front seat of the taxi unless your driver is a woman.

Culture

Culture in Dubai is rich and varied, from desert Bedouin traditions such as storytelling, to contemporary theatre and musical performances. As a multicultural city, visitors can enjoy watching belly dancers from Turkey and Egypt, pop singers from Lebanon and traditional Emirati stick dancing.

Performance art

Music has long been integral to Arabic culture, ever since the days when desert tribes used song as an inspiration for teamwork in their daily tasks. Today, Arabic nightclubs are the main venues for tourists to hear traditional Arabian music, played on instruments such as the Oud, a stringed instrument not dissimilar to the lyre, and watch dance forms that go back centuries. Try the Al-Diwan in the **Metropolitan Palace Hotel** (ⓐ Al-Maktoum Road ❶ 4 227 0000 ⓦ www.methotels.com/metpalace), which features a singer and belly dancer, and the Escoba at the **Al-Khaleej Palace Hotel** (ⓐ Al-Maktoum Road ❶ 223 1000 for details), which claims to be the city's liveliest music venue.

However, Dubai obviously also prides itself on its international reputation, and many hotel bars provide more standard Western-style entertainment, such as jazz bands and pianists. International stars and arts companies also come to perform at the city's state-of-the-art venues – in the recent past artists such as Sting and Tom Jones, and the Reduced Shakespeare Company, have entertained audiences beneath the desert skies.

Visual arts

Middle-Eastern art is a budding cultural field, with artists such as Yassine Belferd and Sarah Khalid, among many others, beginning to attract the attention of international critics. The **Dubai International Art Centre** (📍 Beach Road ☎ 344 4398 🌐 www.artdubai.com) and the Emirates Fine Arts Society (☎ 535 4488 🌐 www.artsuae.org.ae) are the city's most important visual galleries. The former has a more contemporary edge to it, as well as offering workshops, while the latter is dedicated to the promotion of fine-arts graduates from around the Emirates. The Creative Art Centre (📍 Al-Jumeirah Road ☎ 344 4394), is a hive of cultural activity, which runs from Saturday to Wednesday. Mornings are reserved for young children, afternoons for older children and, during winter, evenings are set aside for adult classes. The Sharjah area also has five different centres all dedicated to visual arts (see page 122).

🔽 *Dubai Museum – housed in the Al-Fahidi Fort*

Museums & heritage centres

With its glittering skyline and brash modernity, few people would consider Dubai as a museum destination. Yet, despite thriving under its luxury tourist reputation, the city is certainly keen to preserve its more ancient traditions and culture. The Dubai Museum (see page 83) is probably the most important in terms of its vast collection relating to all manner of Arabic cultural subjects. From the desert to the souk, from warfare to agriculture, nothing is overlooked here in the celebration of Arabian life.

The city has also created several 'heritage villages' and areas that preserve traditional life as a kind of living museum. The Heritage and Diving Village (see page 84) concentrates on the coastal history, including pearl diving (see page 85), but it also a lively centre bustling with folk musicians and craftspeople.

Archaeological sites such as Jumeirah (see page 104) as well as the Archaeological Museum in Sharjah (see page 121) also uncover the secrets of the region's past.

▶ Exploring the souks is a must

Shopping

If you are coming to Dubai just to shop, then plan to visit during January and February when the Dubai Shopping Festival takes place (see page 10). The malls are stacked to the rafters with merchandise, and the souks have many excellent bargains. The highlight of this extravaganza is the Global Village, where more than 70 countries sell everything from Tunisian pottery to delicate Palestinian

BARGAINING

Bargaining is a part of life in Dubai and is an accepted practice, especially in the souks, where vendors expect to drop the price, particularly for cash. Once you get the hang of it, you might even enjoy the process. The key to bargaining is to decide in advance what you are willing to pay for an item and be prepared to walk away if you don't get it for that price. Note, however, that shops in the more upmarket shopping malls do not usually go in for bargaining: the price advertised is the price you will pay.

Some points to keep in mind while bargaining are:

- Always be polite and amiable and never use rudeness or aggression as a bargaining tool.
- To begin, ask the shop assistant the price and, as he tells you, look surprised or uninterested. A rule of thumb is to offer half the quoted price. Then, the game is afoot. The assistant will counter-offer, as will you, until you reach a sum agreeable to both of you.
- Once you have agreed to a price it is taken as a verbal contract and you are expected to buy.

embroidery. The whole city turns out for this festival of consumerism and there are musical events, fireworks and parades. Shopping becomes the focus again during the Dubai Summer Surprises (see page 11). It's not the most sensible time to visit: the thermometer-breaking temperatures are guaranteed to keep you inside the air-conditioned malls.

The newly opened Mall of the Emirates (see page 99) is the latest addition to Dubai's shopping centres, while Deira City Centre (see page 74) is one of Dubai's most popular, with shopping, cinemas and restaurants. Both locals and tourists head for the Burjurman Centre (see page 88) in Bur Dubai for its designer-label shops such as Christian Lacroix and Donna Karan. The Egyptian-themed Wafi City Mall (see page 100) boasts a wide range of designer boutiques, a fitness centre, spa and children's amusement area. If it has to be designer, take your credit card to the Emirates Towers Shopping Boulevard on Sheikh Zayed Road (see page 96), where you'll find more than 40 luxury stores, including Bulgari, Jimmy Choo, Armani and Cartier.

It wouldn't be a proper trip to the Middle East if you didn't at least look at a rug or two. Strike a good deal in Dubai itself or head about 20 minutes from the city to the Central Souk in neighbouring Sharjah. Be prepared to bargain.

If a carpet is too big to stuff into your suitcase, head for the souk in Deira (see page 70). Here, amid the heady aroma of spices and reams of garish fabrics, you can pick up a *dalla* (coffee pot) made of copper, carved wooden or leather-stuffed camels, or a *sheesha* (water pipe) as an authentic memento of your trip.

Don't forget to take a foray into a Dubai supermarket. You could pack your picnic basket with Al-Jazeera coffee, acacia honey, mango or strawberry juice, Iranian caviar – and even packaged camel's milk.

Eating & drinking

Dubai is such a modern, multicultural, technologically advanced place that it is easy to forget how it used to be. The diet of the nomadic Bedouin tribes was very limited by modern standards. They ate little beyond camel meat, camel milk, fish and dates. Even given that there are many different varieties of dates in the region, this doesn't form the basis of an exciting cuisine. Today, however, almost every cuisine imaginable is represented in the city, right down to the grease and salt emporiums of the fast-food chains.

● *Dine by the waterside*

Traditional Arabic cuisine is a blend of many Middle Eastern influences from countries such as Morocco, Tunisia, Egypt and Iran. In Dubai, however, the primary influence is Lebanese. Typical ingredients include chicken, beef, lamb, seafood, rice, nuts, yoghurt and spices.

Popular dishes

Listed below are some of the most popular dishes of the region that can be found on many restaurant menus.

Harees is a simple dish, eaten as a main meal, created by placing small cubes of meat (usually lamb), cracked wheat and water together in a large earthenware pot and then slowly cooking until the meat is tender. The ingredients are then blended together into a porridge-like consistency.

Machboos, another main dish meal, is usually made from lamb or chicken. The meat is boiled together with onions, rice, salt and dried lemons until tender. This concoction is a popular lunchtime dish.

For breakfast try *mohalla*, a flat bread spread with honey and date syrup. To do as the locals do, wash it down with very sweet, very strong coffee.

For those with a sweet tooth, *khabeesah* is a sweet dish composed of roasted flour, water, sugar and saffron, *lukimat* consists of dough balls eaten with date syrup, *assesada* is semolina combined with saffron, while *batheeth* is a dish made of freshly ripened dates in juice. All are a fine way to finish a meal.

The best-known local fish is called *hammour*, a type of grouper. It appears on most restaurant menus and is an excellent entrée.

For a taste of everything order a 'mezze' (also known as mezza, meza and other similar words), a buffet-style meal with plenty of appetisers and appetiser-sized courses all placed on the table at the same time. This is not only an opportunity to sample the wide variety of flavours and cooking techniques, but also lends itself to a more leisurely, less structured way of eating the meal.

Eating out
Eating out is extremely popular in Dubai, and most places buzz with activity, especially at night. Restaurants usually open at around 19.00, but don't get really busy until about 21.00. A speciality is Friday brunch, popular with everyone in the city.

For a particularly unique experience, and to get in the spirit of your desert adventure, why not go for a dune dinner away from the city, or take in the lights of the city from a dinner cruise on the creek?

If you get peckish while walking the streets during the day or early evening, try *shawarma* (a Middle Eastern version of the kebab served in bread) from a roadside vendor, or nibble dates as you wander through the malls.

Special considerations
It is worth remembering that Muslims are forbidden to eat the meat of any animal that has not been slaughtered in accordance with Islamic rituals, known as 'halaal'. Pork is strictly forbidden. Alcohol is also forbidden if you are eating in a local establishment rather than in a hotel or nightclub.

> **RESTAURANT CATEGORIES**
> The following price guide used throughout the book indicates the average price per head for a 2–3 course dinner, excluding drinks.
> **£** up to 35 Dh; **££** 35–135 Dh; **£££** above 135 Dh

SHEESHA PIPES

Throughout the Middle East, smoking the traditional '*sheesha*', or '*nargile*' (water pipe), is a popular and relaxing pastime, usually enjoyed after a meal in a local café while chatting with friends.

The pipes can be smoked with a variety of flavoured tobaccos, such as apple or strawberry.

Take home a sheesha pipe as a souvenir of your trip. They can be readily purchased in shops, including supermarkets.

◓ *Shopping malls offer a range of meal options*

Entertainment & nightlife

Dubai is without a doubt party central of the Gulf, catering to both the young and trendy and the more mature visitor. The best bars are those found in the major hotels.

If nightlife is what you're after, you can't go wrong here, but you'll also have to be prepared for a very late bedtime – most places don't start buzzing until about 23.00. Prior to that, you're likely to be a lone party animal.

MUSIC

Dubai is increasingly attracting major international stars to perform there, lured by glamorous venues and high fees. The dance scene is also active, with top DJs from Europe and the UK guesting at the many nightclubs.

For classical music and ballet, the Dubai International Congress Centre, Dubai World Trade Centre, Bur Dubai (① 331 4200 ⓦ www.dwtc.com) and The Crowne Plaza Hotel (ⓐ Sheikh Zayed Road ① 331 1111) are the main venues hosting visiting orchestras and solo musicians from around the world, including touring shows such as Michael Flatley's 'Riverdance'. Many hotels employ talented pianists, harpists and lounge singers.

Arabic nightclubs are the main venues for traditional Arabian music and belly dancing (see page 24).

THEATRE

Not so long ago, the only theatre you could find in Dubai would be the British Airways Playhouse presented in the ballroom of the InterContinental Hotel. This touring company staged a changing programme of classics, contemporary plays and comedies to a largely expat audience. Today, however, the theatrical landscape of the city has expanded considerably.

The Indian Playhouse in the InterContinental Hotel (☎ 222 7171) features performances by Burjor Patel Productions. The British Touring Shakespeare Company (ⓦ www.britishtouringshakespeare.co.uk) brings the works of the great bard to the Gulf on a regular basis. Works by playwrights such as Neil Simon and Tom Stoppard, as well as musicals and a Christmas pantomime, are presented by the Dubai Drama Group (☎ 333 1155 ⓦ www.dubaidramagroup.org), a long-standing amateur theatrical company. Meanwhile the much-anticipated Dubai Community Theatre & Arts Centre, with seats for more than 500, is due to open at the end of 2006 (see page 96).

FILM

From Hollywood to Bollywood, cinema is huge in Dubai. There are a number of cinemas for one to choose from, including Al-Massa Bustan (ⓐ Al-Bustan Centre ☎ 263 3444 ⓦ www.al-bustan.com) and Grand Cineplex, adjacent to Wafi City (☎ 324 0000), which provide English-language films. Big-budget Hollywood blockbusters are the mainstay – you're not likely to find much call for arty independent movies in this larger-than-life city.

LISTINGS

The monthly *Time Out* magazine, which can be found in many hotels, provides information on events and performances in Dubai. Time Out also sells tickets for events (☎ 800 4669 ⓦ www.itp.net/tickets).

Sport & relaxation

One of the biggest draws for visitors to Dubai are the excellent sport and leisure facilities that it offers – a booming trade that is proven by the new hotels and sports centres that open up at remarkable speed. From golf courses to sand skiing, the city offers plenty of ways to participate in your favourite sport.

Camel racing is a very popular spectator pastime in the Emirates. The sheer spectacle of diminutive jockeys, usually from India or Bangladesh, perched atop one of these gambolling 'ships of the desert', was a sight to behold, though since 2005 the UAE has used robot jockeys instead of children. Races are held early on Thursday and Friday mornings during the winter and spring.

Dubai is also a Mecca for horse-racing enthusiasts. The Dubai World Cup is the richest horse race in the world, with the purse

● *Camel racing using robot jockeys*

exceeding $US 15 million. Officially, gambling is forbidden by the laws of Islam, but this is a tolerant place, and plenty of betting takes place. The racing season lasts from November until March, with most races being held in the cooler evening hours.

Motor sports are also popular as entertainment for both spectators and participants in Dubai. From wadi-bashing on a weekend in 4WD vehicles to the excitement of the FIA Cross-Country Rally World Cup, and hopefully, in the future, a Formula 1 event, it's clear that the roar of an engine is something that locals and visitors alike enjoy.

Last but not least, the spectacular Ski Dubai in Mall of the Emirates, the third-largest indoor centre in the world, includes a revolving ski slope, ice bridge, cable lift, and slopes for all ages and abilities. ⓦ www.skidubai.com ⓛ 10.00–23.00 Sat–Tues, 10.00–24.00 Wed–Fri

SPAS

With its reputation as a luxury resort it would seem fairly obvious that Dubai would put heavy emphasis on the spa industry. There are a number of excellent spas that offer a wide range of treatments to leave you feeling and looking your best.

In addition, with its position on the threshold between East and West, many of the treatments and techniques merge those of diverse cultures. Use your time to experience such varied therapies as Rasul or Hamman, a steam-cleansing ritual from Morocco.

Al-Asalla Spa

This ladies-only spa is a pampering heaven, with traditional regimes firmly rooted in Eastern culture combined with modern therapies such as Vichy showers. Immerse yourself in luxury and imagine

yourself back in the grand Sheikh palaces of old. ⓐ Dubai Ladies
Club, Jumeirah Beach Road ⓣ 349 9922 ⓦ www.dubailadiesclub.com

Cleopatra's Spa & Health Club

As its name suggests there's more than a nod to Ancient Egypt
here, but that's not to say that you'll miss out on the best modern
treatments. While you may not be able to enjoy a milk bath like
the great queen herself, you can experience Ayurveda, Rasul,
Ionithermie, Light Therapy and all manner of wraps and rituals.
ⓐ Pyramids, Wafi City, off Oud Metha Road ⓣ 324 7700
ⓦ www.cleopatras-spa.com

Givenchy Spa

Tranquillity is the word here – indulge in a massage on the
heated marble table, open your pores in the steam rooms, relax
in the whirlpool, then finish off with a new hairdo in the salon
ready for a night out. ⓐ One & Only Royal Mirage, Al-Sufouh Road
ⓣ 399 9999 ⓦ www.oneandonlyresorts.com/flash.html

The Grand Spa

If all that lounging around has got to you, this is the place to come
to stretch some muscles. On-site facilities include a 20-m pool,
state-of-the-art gymnasium, squash courts, juice bar and plunge
pools. There is also a tennis centre and a 450-m (1,476-ft) jogging
track. ⓐ Grand Hyatt Dubai, Al-Qutaeyat Road ⓣ 317 1234
ⓦ www.dubai.grand.hyatt.com

The Oasis Retreat Spa

You can opt for the gentle kneading of a Western massage here or
commit yourself to the more deep-rooted pummelling of a Balinese

massage, depending how many aches and pains you want to be rid of. ➊ Oasis Beach Hotel, Jumeirah Beach Road ➊ 399 4444

Satori Spa

Another opportunity for Balinese massages, as well as other Eastern offerings including reviving ginger tea. Close your eyes and imagine yourself in a tropical paradise. ➊ Jumeirah Beach Club Resort & Spa ➊ 344 5333 ➊ www.jumeirahbeachclub.com/lifestyle

Willow Stream Spa

The ninth floor of the Fairmont hotel is one of the best-known spa areas in Dubai, with two swimming pools, indoor and outdoor Jacuzzi, aerobic classes and a fully equipped fitness centre.
➊ Fairmont Dubai, Sheikh Zayed Road ➊ 311 8800
➊ http://www.fairmont.com/dubai

SPA ETIQUETTE

Although nothing is set in stone, here are some useful bits of advice if you're planning a spa visit.

- Arrive 15–20 minutes prior to your appointment – this not only gives you time to change at leisure but also confirms to the spa staff that you haven't cancelled.
- Leave your mobile phone behind or switch it off – it can really disturb a calming massage.
- You will have to remove jewellery for treatments, so it is best to leave it in your hotel room (preferably in the safe).
- Remember this is an Islamic country – swimsuits (not bikinis) should be worn in 'wet' areas.

TEE-TIME IN DUBAI

Care for a round of golf? Dubai is one of the world's premier golfing destinations, with top-class facilities and excellent weather all year round. There are already quite a few international standard golf courses within the city and several more are in the planning stages. Each year the city is host to the prestigious Dubai Desert Classic, which attracts the top names in the game, and is played at the Emirates Golf Club.

Dubai Country Club

Both a 9- and 18-hole course on sand. ⓐ Al-Awir ⓣ 333 1155
ⓦ www.dubaicountryclub.com ⓛ 08.00–22.00

Dubai Creek Golf & Yacht Club

Par 71, 18-hole championship golf course, which has hosted the Desert Classic. ⓐ Garhoud ⓣ 295 6000 ⓦ www.dubaigolf.com
ⓛ 06.30–19.00

Emirates Golf Club

Courses offer challenging but fair golf to all standards of players. The Majlis is an 18-hole course that plays to a par of 72. The Wadi, also an 18-hole course, plays to a par of 72. ⓐ Sheikh Zayed Road
ⓣ 380 2222 ⓦ www.dubaigolf.com ⓛ 06.00–24.00

Hatta Fort Golf Courses

Standard play courses suitable for all levels of player. ⓐ 100 km
(62 miles) from Dubai towards the east ⓣ 852 3211
ⓦ www.jebelalihotel.com

Nad Al-Sheba Club

Scottish Links-style 18-hole course. The only floodlit course
in the Middle East. ⓐ off Dubai Al-Ain Road ⓣ 336 3666
ⓦ www.nadalshebaclub.com ⓛ 07.00–24.00

The Resort Golf Course

A 9-hole, par-36 course with terrific views of the Gulf, and peacocks
that meander over the course. ⓐ Jebel Ali Golf Resort & Spa, Jebel Ali
ⓣ 883 6000 ⓦ www.jebelali-international.com

ⓞ *Dubai Creek Golf Club*

Accommodation

Dubai justifiably has a reputation for luxury – it is, after all, home to the only 7-star hotel, the Burj Al Arab, in the world. But that doesn't mean that if you want to travel on a shoestring you must cross Dubai off your list. There are many budget and modest options from which to choose.

It's also worth noting that during Ramadan (see page 15), when the number of visitors significantly decreases, many of the upmarket and luxury hotels will decrease room rates by as much as 50 per cent. If you can go with the flow of this important religious holiday and not eat, drink or smoke in public until after sundown, you can score a great deal.

HOTELS

Al-Arraf Hotel £ A no-frills option, but the friendliness of the staff more than makes up for the basic surroundings. ⓐ Deira, near the Gold Souk, 12 km (7½ miles) from the airport ⓣ 4 225 0700

Al-Khayam Hotel £ A small, basic hotel close to the Gold Souk. Not recommended for single women because of its location, but other than that, a good budget option. ⓐ Sikkat Al-Khail Street, Deira ⓣ 4 226 4211

Deira Palace Hotel £ Probably the most popular budget option in the city – which means booking well ahead of your trip. Clean and functional. ⓐ 67 St Deira ⓣ 4 229 0120

Dubai Youth Hostel £ This really is for travellers on a shoestring or less, although the new block features en-suite rooms,

a fridge and air conditioning. There is also a cafeteria.
🅐 39 Al-Nahda Road, Deira ☏ 4 298 8161 ⓦ www.hostelsweb.com

Dallas Hotel £–££ Good value in an otherwise quite pricey location. Rooms are en-suite, although bathroom facilities are basic. 🅐 Bur Dubai ☏ 4 351 1223

Admiral Plaza ££ Tastefully designed rooms feature air conditioning, satellite TV, tea- and coffee-making facilities, and a minibar. The hotel also has a coffee shop and an English pub on site.
🅐 Al-Nahada Street, Bur Dubai ☏ 4 393 5333

Al-Bustan Rotana ££ Catering largely to a business clientele, but at an unusually good price. Facilities include a gym, squash courts and a children's play area. On-site restaurants include Benihana (Japanese) and The Blue Elephant (Thai). 🅐 Casablanca Road, Al-Garhoud, Deira ☏ 4 282 0000 ⓦ www.rotana.com

Ambassador ££ Another hotel catering to the less flashy side of the business market. There are all the usual facilities, including internet connection. If you're feeling homesick, the on-site George & Dragon Pub attempts to bring a bit of Britain to the desert. 🅐 Al-Falah Street, Bur Dubai ☏ 4 393 9444 ⓦ www.astamb.com

> **PRICE RATINGS**
> Hotels in this book are graded according to the average price for a double room per night.
> £ up to 300 Dh; ££ 300–600 Dh; £££ above 600 Dh

Ibis World Trade Centre ££ The rooms are a little on the small side, but they're air conditioned, have satellite TV and, with such a central location, they're great value for money. The breakfast choice is so vast it will set you up for the rest of the day – a good choice during Ramadan, then. ⓐ Sheikh Zayed Road ❶ 4 332 4444 ⓦ www.ibishotels.com

Marco Polo Hotel ££ Decent facilities, roomy rooms (including 12 suites) and a good on-site Mexican restaurant. Transfers to and from the airport, 15 minutes away, are included in the price. ⓐ Al-Muteena Street, Deira ❶ 4 272 0000 ⓦ www.marcopolohotel.net/main.html

Phoenicia ££ There's a definitive retro feel to the décor here, with bold, brash primary colours gracing the walls. Makes a change from the impersonal feel of most business hotels. ⓐ Al-Nasr Square, Deira ❶ 4 222 7191 ⓦ www.phoeniciahoteldubai.com

Quality Inn Horizon ££ Part of an international chain, so don't expect individuality here, but there are all the mod cons including spacious rooms with air conditioning and satellite TV. The concierge facility in reception is great if you want to have day trips organised for you. A free airport shuttle is also available. ⓐ Al-Rigga Road, Deira ❶ 4 227 1919

Regal Plaza Hotel ££ Smallish rooms but nicely decorated and furnished. The sports bar, Goodfellas, is always a lively place for a drink, attracting guests and expats. ⓐ Al-Mankhool Road, Bur Dubai ❶ 4 355 6633 ⓦ www.ramee-group.com/ramee/regal.html

Riviera Hotel ££ If a view of the Creek is your desire, this is the place to watch the waterfront activity. The rooms are well furnished and comfortable, with minibar and satellite TV, and there's also an on-site business centre for that vital email or fax.
ⓐ Baniyas Street, Deira ⓣ 4 222 2131 ⓦ www.rivierahotel-dubai.com

Seashell Inn Dubai ££ Good value all year round, but between April and August it's even better as room tariffs reduce by 50 per cent. The en-suite facilities aren't always what they might be, but the staff are friendly and, for night-owls, there's an on-site disco.
ⓐ Khalid Bin Waleed Road, Bur Dubai ⓣ 4 393 4777

Vendome Plaza Hotel ££ The whitewashed rooms don't create much of an atmosphere here, but it's a central location and the staff are welcoming. ⓐ Al-Rigga Road, Deira ⓣ 4 222 2333

⬤ *Wallow in luxury at the Fairmont Hotel, Dubai*

XVA Gallery ££ The third floor above the art gallery contains a tiny hotel that will appeal to anyone with an eye for the unusual and the bohemian. Each room is decorated in a different style, and the location in the Bastakiya quarter (see page 80) is an added attraction. **ⓐ** 15a St Bastakiya, Bur Dubai **ⓣ** 4 353 5383 **ⓦ** www.xvagallery.com

Ascot £££ Opened in 2003 this hotel has quickly become a popular option with UK business travellers and holidaymakers, and not just because of its name. There's a fitness centre, conference facilities and two restaurants – Yakitori (Japanese) and Troika (Russian). **ⓐ** Khalid Bin Al-Walid Road, Bur Dubai **ⓣ** 4 352 0900

Burj Al-Arab £££ The world's only 7-star hotel and a Dubai landmark certainly lives up to its reputation. The rooms (all suites) decorated in silks and velvets are so sumptuous you'll feel like Arab royalty, but there are also high-tech facilities such as laptops in each. One of the restaurants is centred round a vast, circular aquarium. The ultimate hotel experience. **ⓐ** Jumeirah **ⓣ** 4 301 7777 **ⓦ** www.burj-al-arab.com

Crowne Plaza Dubai £££ The largest hotel in the city (560 rooms) doesn't always lend itself to personal service but it's dripping in luxury. There's a health club, including spa and pool, shopping mall, ten restaurants and even an Arabian *majlis* for entertaining local guests. **ⓐ** Sheikh Zayed Al-Nahyan Road **ⓣ** 4 331 1111 **ⓦ** www.ichotelsgroup.com

Emirates Tower £££ Luxury is combined with high-tech here, although the rooms' functions are so automated it can get confusing as to which button to press when. A great option for single women travellers as there's a women-only floor. ❸ Sheikh Zayed Road ❶ 4 330 0000 ❿ www.jumeirahemiratestowers.com

Fairmont Hotel Dubai £££ A Dubai stalwart for both business and leisure travellers. Offers a large choice of restaurants and bars, a beautiful Roman-style health club and spa, and wonderful vistas of the city from rooms on the upper floors. ❸ Sheikh Zayed Road ❶ 4 332 5555 ❿ www.fairmont.com

Hyatt Regency Dubai £££ Located on the Deira Corniche across from the Gold Souk, the facilities here are so all-encompassing that it would be impossible to mention them all. Suffice to say, whatever you need, you'll find it here. It also boasts Dubai's only revolving restaurant, with great views of the Gulf. ❸ Corniche Alkhaleej Road, Deira ❶ 4 209 1234 ❿ www.dubai.regency.hyatt.com

InterContinental Dubai £££ The InterContinental kicked off the luxury hotel trade in Dubai and, although it's now been somewhat surpassed by its rivals, it's still a great choice for business travellers (there are ten meeting rooms) and sports enthusiasts (pool, squash courts, tennis courts). ❸ Bin Yas Street, Deira ❶ 4 222 7171 ❿ www.dubai.intercontinental.com/

Shangri-La £££ Looming above the palm trees, with great views of the Gulf, the Shangri-La combines luxury and style with richly decorated rooms. There's also the option of apartment accommodation, offering a little more privacy and independence. ❸ Sheikh Zayed Road ❶ 4 343 8888 ❿ www.shangri-la.com

THE BEST OF DUBAI

TOP 10 ATTRACTIONS

- **Shopping Malls** Shopaholics from all over the world flock to these air-conditioned emporiums filled with all the designer names you could wish for.

- **Bastakiya** This is a rare glimpse of 'Old Dubai', filled with winding lanes and secluded courtyards: a taste of real Arabic life (see page 80).

- **Wild Wadi Water Park** A kids' paradise of pools and water slides, as well as smart sunbathing areas for the adults (see page 110).

- **Ski Dubai** It may seem incongruous, but the first indoor ski resort in the Middle East has proved an unparalleled success. The artificial slopes are crowded with fashionistas (see pages 37 & 54).

- **Dubai Museum** Everything you ever needed to know about the history of Dubai can be found here, from its tribal heritage to the skyscraping luxury of today (see page 83).

- **Desert Safaris** Head out into the desert and eat and sleep in a genuine Bedouin tent. Running, driving and skiing down the dunes is also a thrill not to be missed (see page 116).

- **The Souks** Whether you're after gold, spices or electronics, you're bound to find what you desire in the dark, aromatic alleyways of these markets (see page 70).

- **Sharjah** The carpet and cultural capital of the UAE, about 20 minutes outside the city. Don't miss the Blue Souk, named after the cerulean tiles decorating the market's walls (see page 124).

- **Burj Al-Arab** Dubai's most recognisable building dominates the coastline. Inside is probably one of the most luxurious hotels in the world (see page 46).

- **The Creek** Cutting through the old and new districts of Dubai, this waterway makes it clear why the city has had such a successful trading heritage. A boat trip on a dhow makes for a relaxing afternoon (see page 64).

▼ *See the city from the water*

Depending on the time you have, here are some short itineraries, helping you tap into the best of Dubai.

HALF-DAY: DUBAI IN A HURRY

Immerse yourself in the bustle of the Deira district by beginning your adventure along the Creek. This is the business district and soul of the city – the area that would make Dubai its fortune in the second half of the 20th century.

Next it's time to bargain your way through the souk (see page 70) of your choice for an authentic Arab experience.

Then head to the Grand Mosque (see page 84), passing through the historic Bastakiya neighbourhood (see page 80). Take time to nibble some local delicacies such as *shawarma* (see page 32) from a street vendor, or some dates and Lebanese sweets.

Complete your adventure with an Arabian-style dinner and perhaps even try a *sheesha* pipe (see page 33).

1 DAY: TIME TO SEE A LITTLE MORE

Pay a visit to the Dubai Museum (see page 83) to gain an historical perspective of the city. From the museum it's an easy stroll to Sheikh Saeed al-Maktoum House, an excellent place to see the traditional architecture of the city (see page 86). For more historical background visit the oldest school in Dubai, Al-Ahmadiya School (see page 64), or stop at the Heritage Village (see page 84) for a glimpse of how Dubai lived a short century ago.

A good way to see more of Dubai is to take a Big Bus Company tour of the city. Eight double-decker buses follow two routes through the city (to the beach and back) all day between 09.00 and 17.00. The open-top vehicles make 19 stops throughout the city, allowing you to hop on and off at your whim. Buses depart from Wafi City every hour and a half.

Make time for a shopping expedition at the Mall of the Emirates (see page 99) or the Mercato in Jumeirah (see page 108). And no trip to Dubai would be complete without a visit to the Burj Al-Arab, the only 7-star hotel in the world. Visitors are allowed to have a drink at the bar or enjoy dinner at the hotel (see page 46).

2–3 DAYS: SHORT CITY BREAK

With more time you can explore many of the different neighbourhoods or visit the sights outside the city such as the Hatta Rock Pools (see page 116) or even spend a day in the desert engaging in some 4WD wadi bashing or sand-dune skiing (see page 117).

Depending upon the time of year, go to see the camel or horse races (see pages 36–7), take in a round of golf (see page 40) or visit Sharjah, a neighbouring Emirate, to shop at the Blue Souk for a carpet (see page 124).

LONGER: ENJOYING DUBAI TO THE FULL

With additional time in the region you can truly experience the depth of variety available in this desert paradise. Extra days will also give you plenty of time to explore destinations that are further afield, such as Muscat, the capital of Oman, which will perhaps be the next Dubai (see page 134). Or take a trip to Fujairah, one of the most beautiful areas of the UAE, boasting rugged mountains, spectacular waterfalls, superb beaches and fantastic watersports (see page 128).

Something for nothing

Despite its reputation for luxury, it is very easy to spend a day or two in Dubai without putting your hand in your wallet too frequently. The Creekside, with its dhows and *abras* plying the waters, has a wonderful atmosphere that can immerse you for hours, while the

⬤ *Dubai's first school: the Al-Ahmadiya*

soft sand beaches of Jumeirah are one of the city's main draws and entirely free to enjoy.

During the hectic months of the Dubai Shopping Festival (see page 10), evening parades and displays of fireworks light up the night and there are many free concerts and performances held at various venues around the city.

On the tourist trail, the Al-Ahmadiya School (see page 64) – where sheikhs sent their sons to be educated – and Heritage House (see page 68) are two of Dubai's most notable historic landmarks.

The experience of the souks is free – there's no obligation to buy. The sights, sounds, aromas and tastes alone will fill your senses with the wonder of the Eastern marketplace. You're likely to be tempted, of course, by the well-honed patter of the vendors, but you can politely walk away if you don't want to buy.

Soak up the arts at The Courtyard (see page 96). This fairly eccentric cultural centre is filled with buildings designed to interpret construction styles from around the world. An Islamic entry, for example, merges with a Moorish façade that will lead you to an Egyptian tomb. The exhibitions of artists from around the world match the variety of the architecture.

The literary-minded can immerse themselves in Arabia's wealth of writings at the Sultan Bin Ali Al-Owais Cultural Foundation's library (see page 73). With more than 40,000 volumes available, a world of poetry, literature, history and philosophy is yours to enjoy in the calm and quiet reading hall, all free of charge.

When the temperature soars

During the summer months of June, July, August and even into
September, the temperature of Dubai can soar well above 40°C
(104°F), sending both tourists and locals fleeing to the air-
conditioned confines of indoor activities. When the Dubai
International Airport first opened several decades ago it was
frequently filled in the evenings. The main attraction? It was one of
the first public buildings to offer air conditioning.

Today, with a wide choice of huge shopping malls all cooled to a
comfortable temperature, there's no need to travel to the airport
just to seek a drop in the temperature. The malls of Dubai feature all
kinds of shopping, food options, entertainment, cinemas and play
areas for children.

Ski Dubai off Sheikh Zayed Road is, of course, absolutely the
coolest place in the city and not just because of the 'snow'. This
indoor ski slope is one of the largest in the world, using snow made
in the same way that artificial snow is created for outdoor resorts.
So, go ahead, escape the blazing heat outside and chill out with
some skiing, snowboarding or good old-fashioned tobogganing. Ski
Dubai will soon be joined by the Dubai Sunny Mountain Ski Dome,
planned as a feature of Dubailand (see page 113).

If skiing is a little too energetic for you, try taking to the ice at
the skating rink in the Hyatt Regency hotel (see page 47). Skates are
available to hire and there are even lessons to help you improve or
teach you how it's done.

Wild Wadi Water Park (see page 110) is a great place to lower your
body temperature by plunging into one of the largest water parks in
the world. Twenty-four rides are all interconnected so you can hop
off one and onto another and never spend a dry moment all day.

The rides vary from the scream-inducing plunge drops to sedate wave pools.

The Gold & Diamond Park & Museum on Sheikh Zayed Road will save you from the heat, but no guarantees about any damage to your wallet. Take a tour of the jewellery manufacturing plant to learn how baubles, bangles and beads are created (see page 95).

🔺 *From hot to not: the amazing Ski Dubai*

On arrival

TIME DIFFERENCES

Dubai is four hours ahead of London (Greenwich Mean Time) and the clocks do not change throughout the year. It is eight hours ahead of New York and Toronto, nine ahead of Chicago, eleven ahead of San Francisco and Vancouver, six behind Sydney, eight behind Wellington and two ahead of Johannesburg.

ARRIVING

The Dubai International Airport sets the tone of your trip to the city and environs immediately upon arrival. This modern, state-of-the-art facility is everything an international airport should be. Round-the-clock amenities include duty free, hotel and apartment reservation services, tourist information, ATM and money exchange, car rental, taxis and cafés.

When it's time to leave Dubai, if you haven't had your fill of shopping in the city's malls, the departure halls are filled with an abundance of luxury goods and the duty free is top notch in both supply and variety.

By Air

Airlines flying to Dubai:

Air France ☎ 359 1000 🌐 www.airfrance.com
Al-Italia ☎ 544 8259 🌐 www.alitalia.com
British Airways ☎ 850 9850 🌐 www.britishairways.com
Emirates ☎ 243 2222 🌐 www.emirates.com
Etihad ☎ 241 7121 🌐 www.etihadairways.com
KLM ☎ 507 4047 🌐 www.klm.com
Kuwait Airways ☎ 741 2007 🌐 www.kuwait-airways.com

Lufthansa ☎ 773 7747 🌐 www.lufthansa.com
Malaysian Airways ☎ 607 9090 🌐 www.malaysiaairlines.com
Olympic Airways ☎ 606 0460 🌐 www.olympicairlines.com
Qatar Airways ☎ 789 63636 🌐 www.qatarairways.com
Swiss ☎ 601 0956 🌐 www.swiss.com
Turkish Airlines ☎ 776 9300 🌐 www.thy.com

🔺 *Dubai International Airport*

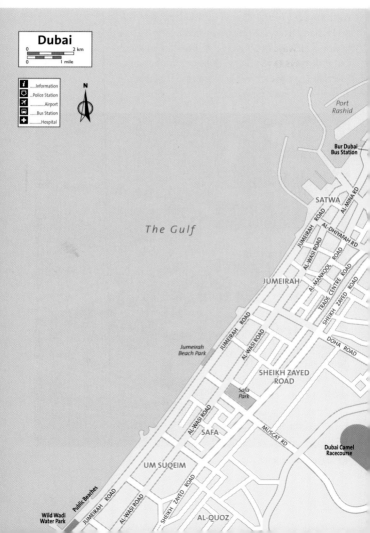

Dubai

0 ___ 2 km
0 ___ 1 mile

- *i* ......Information
- .....Police Station
- ....Airport
- .....Bus Station
- ....Hospital

N

Port Rashid

Bur Dubai Bus Station

SATWA

AL-MINA RD

JUMEIRAH ROAD

AL-DHIYAFAH RD

AL-WASL ROAD

AL-MANKOOL ROAD

TRADE CENTRE ROAD

The Gulf

JUMEIRAH

SHEIKH ZAYED ROAD

DOHA ROAD

JUMEIRAH ROAD

Jumeirah Beach Park

AL-WASL ROAD

SHEIKH ZAYED ROAD

Safa Park

MUSCAT RD

AL-WASL ROAD

SAFA

Dubai Camel Racecourse

UM SUQEIM

Public Beaches

JUMEIRAH ROAD

AL-WASL ROAD

SHEIKH ZAYED ROAD

Wild Wadi Water Park

AL-QUOZ

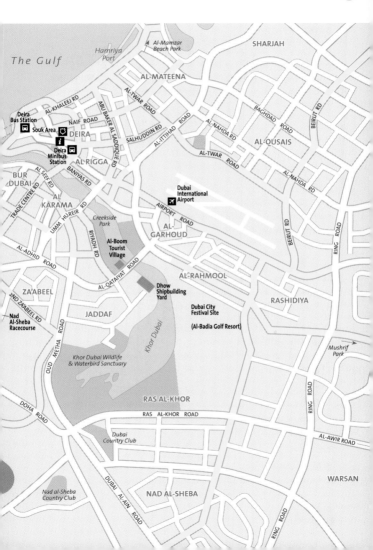

ORIENTATION

Greater Dubai encompasses the areas of Deira, Bur Dubai, Sheikh Zayed Road and Jumeirah spreading both east and west along the Gulf of Arabia. The core of the city is bisected by the Creek, an inlet lined on both sides with dhows, trading ships and new constructions. There are three ways to cross the Creek. You may take a water taxi or *abra*, or cross via the Al-Maktoum Bridge or the Al-Shindaga Tunnel. Jumeirah, with its beautiful beaches, lies to the west and the airport is to the south.

The maps in this book show all the main streets and sights in each area, but many of the restaurants and shops that we list are on smaller streets for which you may need a more detailed map. If you plan to stay in Dubai for more than just a few days it would be wise to invest in a map from a local bookshop, newsstand or tourist board.

GETTING AROUND

Buses run between Dubai International Airport and Deira Bus Station every half an hour. Dubai Transport taxis, recognisable by their light-brown bodywork, also run metered services between the airport and the city centre.

Once in the city, the easiest way to get around Dubai is by taxi or private car. The public bus route is growing but it cannot begin to compare with the metropolitan systems of most European capitals.

Dubai has a large fleet of metered taxis, and fares begin at Dh 3 plus Dh 1.43 for each km.

Expect to pay more for taxi services after 22.00. There are still a few unmetered taxis in the city and, if using one of these, you'll need to haggle over the fare. But it's best to avoid an unmetered taxi unless you crave adventure in all aspects of your life.

If you do want to travel by bus, they run through the city with terminus points at Deira Bus Station, near the Gold Souk, and the Bur Dubai Bus Station on Al-Ghubaiba Road. Passengers can obtain bus times, details about fares and connecting services by calling ☎ freephone 800 4848 between 06.00 and 22.00, seven days a week ⓦ www.dm.gov.ae

If you're visiting the older districts of the city such as Bastakiya (see page 80), the only way to get a real flavour of the alleyways and lanes is on foot. And don't forget the waterway – a trip on a dhow down the Creek is one of the city's most pleasant experiences.

🔺 *Get your dirhams here*

DRIVING

Driving in the city of Dubai is not for the faint of heart. The local drivers are at best aggressive, at worst eccentric. If you do want to rent a car, you will need a credit card and your passport as proof of identity. Despite the erratic style of its drivers, Dubai's road network is comprehensive and orderly and connects all outlying areas. There is also a tunnel and two road bridges that allow drivers to cross from one side of the Creek to the other. Heading out of the city is also straightforward, with well-maintained roads and a motorway to Abu Dhabi.

Unsurprisingly in a city with a strict alcohol code, drinking and driving is taken very seriously indeed – if caught, you'll not only be heavily fined but likely to find yourself behind bars for a short length of time. All accidents, even if it's just a prang, must be reported to the police by law.

CAR HIRE

Avis ⓐ Arrivals Terminal, Dubai International Airport
ⓣ 224 5219 ⓦ www.avis.com

Budget ⓐ Dubai International Airport ⓣ 224 5192
ⓦ www.budgetrentacar.com

Dollar ⓐ World Trade Centre, Sheikh Zayed Road
ⓣ 331 8623 ⓦ www.dollar.com

Fast ⓐ Sahara Tower, Sheikh Zayed Road ⓣ 332 8988
ⓦ www.fastuae.com

Hertz ⓐ Terminal 1, Dubai International Airport, Al-Garoud
ⓣ 224 5222 ⓦ www.hertz.com

▶ *See the sights from an* abra

Deira

Dubai Creek (Khor Dubai), the waterway that bisects Dubai, is really the reason that the city exists. It enabled trade from the earliest days and is still a bustling centrepiece of the city. On the side of the Dhow Wharfage there's still an almost Third World feel to the area, with boxes of fruit, tennis shoes and the odd discarded fridge or washing machine lining the banks waiting to be loaded onto one vessel or another. The other side, however, presents a gleaming skyline of modern, dramatic buildings. Cliché it may be, but this really is an area where East meets West. Ships still ply the ancient trading routes between Asia and Africa and Europe.

The best way to view this dynamic scenario is from the water itself. On the Deira side of the Creek a broad, well-lit promenade extends from the Corniche, allowing visitors to stroll along the coast of the Arabian Gulf. Or, for a nominal sum, small water taxis called *abras* crisscross the Creek from the souks of Deira to the Bur Dubai side.

SIGHTS & ATTRACTIONS

Al-Ahmadiya School

Formal education among Arab tribal societies is a fairly recent consideration in comparison to Western societies, so Dubai's oldest school only dates from 1912. However, the building, constructed under the orders of a wealthy pearl merchant and used by the city's wealthy offspring until the 1950s, is of considerable architectural significance in a city that has lost so many of its historic areas. The school opened as a museum in 2000. Beautifully restored, inside there are now interactive exhibits that explain the history of the

building and the school, while outside traditional homes built out of coral and gypsum are on display. ⓐ Al-Khor Street ❶ 4 226 0286 ⏱ 08.00–19.30 Sat–Thur, 14.30–19.30 Fri; 09.00–16.30 Sat–Thur (during Ramadan), 14.00–16.30 Fri (during Ramadan); admission free

Al-Mamzar Beach Park

If you want to cool off in the heat with the added advantage of formal facilities, head for Al-Mamzar where there are lifeguards on duty, as well as swimming pools, changing rooms and beach chalets. There are also numerous picnic areas with barbecue facilities and a children's play area. The large amphitheatre in the park also hosts evening concerts.

ⓐ On the Gulf shores, north of Al-Hamriya Port ❶ 4 296 6201 ⓦ vgn.dm.gov.ae ⏱ 08.00–22.00, women and children only Wed; admission charge

Deira Fish Market

You don't really need directions to this market – the smell alone will lure you in. The day's catch of fish and shellfish glisten on their icy displays from early morning, waiting to be gutted, filleted and weighed before they hit local dinner tables at night. ⓐ Near the Gold Souk on Sikkat Al-Khali Street

Dhow Shipbuilding Yard

About 1 km (½ mile) south of Al-Gharoud Bridge, the traditional Arab dhows are still built in the historic way. In contrast to the Western method of shipbuilding, dhows are built from the outside in, the carcass completed before the internal frame is added. The teak and shesham woods are also still carved and manipulated by hand not machinery, making them incredibly sturdy and long lasting.

However, these days they make a nod to technology by having engines installed rather than relying on good winds to fill their sails.

ⓐ On Dubai Creek waterfront about 1 km (½ mile) south of Al-Gharhoud Bridge in the Jaddaf district – Dock No 1

🔺 *A traditional dhow*

Dhow Wharfage

If you have always thought that Dubai is just sky-scraping luxury hotels, you're in for a surprise here. This is the beating pulse of the city and has been for centuries – the focal point of water-faring trade ships that have long used Dubai as a strategic port between East and West. A walk along the creek, where traditional dhows still bob at their moorings and cargo still waits to be loaded for its final destination, is one of the most atmospheric experiences of the city, full of Arabic chaos and charm.

ⓐ Deira side of Dubai Creek

Heritage House

This late 19th-century house was the former home of an Iranian merchant and has today been preserved to show how life might have been like for the wealthy at that time. Rooms such as the kitchen, bedroom, two separate *majlis* (meeting rooms) for men and women, and a bridal chamber have been lovingly re-created to offer visitors a sense of upper-class life in days gone by.

ⓐ Al-Ras area of Deira ⓣ 4 226 0286 ⓛ 07.30–14.30 Sat–Wed; 09.00–17.00 Sat–Thur, 14.00–17.00 Fri (Ramadan); admission free

Mushrif Park

The largest public park in the Emirates is an incongruous slab of greenery amid the more usual landscape of desert sands. The big attraction is the **World Village** – an authentic reproduction of buildings from around the world, all cleverly constructed in miniature. One minute you'll be a giant in Tudor England, with thatched and beamed houses at your feet, the next you'll be among Dutch windmills or admiring the intricacy of Balinese temples. There are also two swimming pools in the park (one for men, one for women) and it makes for a lovely place to enjoy a kebab picnic in the sun.

🚉 15 km (9¼ miles) away from Dubai's centre on the road leading to Al-Khawanij ❶ 4 288 3624 ⓦ vgn.dm.gov.ae ❶ 08.00–22.30 Sat–Wed, 08.00–23.30 Thur & Fri; admission charge

BIRDWATCHING

Serious twitchers and enthusiastic amateurs have plenty to write home about in the northern Emirates. There are three major wetlands on the Gulf coast, which are home to a fantastic range of palearctic shorebirds.

The best place for birdwatching, now a designated wildlife sanctuary, is the Khor Dubai Lagoon, which can be visited if you obtain a permit from the police – the area is patrolled year round. The most important birds here are the Greater Flamingoes, but you'll also have the opportunity to look out for the Great White Egret, Spoonbill, Marsh Harrier, Spotted Eagle, Osprey and Caspian Tern.

Mushrif Park (see opposite) is home to Bruce's Scops Owl and the Yellow-throated Sparrow.

Golf courses are excellent places to bird watch, and the Emirates Golf Club is where you might find the Isabelline Shrike, Pintail Snipe, Chestnut-bellied Sandgrouse and Red-wattled Lapwing. Note, however, you need permission from the club to enter.

The Jebel Ali area is rich with White-cheeked Bulbuls, Purple Sunbirds, Hoopoe Larks and Socotra Cormorants.

In Hatta you can spend time watching for the Little Green Bee-eater, Scrub Warbler, Desert Larks, Sand Partridge, the Lappet-faced Vulture and Bonelli's Eagle.

Souk area

These souks (markets) are one of the most traditional and atmospheric experiences of a trip to Dubai and sell everything from rugs to spices, perfumes, and the most precious commodity of all – gold. You'll find all the souks within a stone's throw of the Creek. Forget about the smart shopping malls for the time being – sharpen your bargaining skills and begin your quest for the perfect souvenir of your trip.

ⓐ Both sides of the Creek, in Deira and Bur Dubai 🕐 07.00–12.00 & 17.00–19.00 Sat–Thur, 17.00–19.00 Fri

Deira Covered Souk A good old-fashioned souk touting everything from textiles to kitchenware. It opens early in the morning and then again in the early evening.

ⓐ Al-Sabkha Road

Deira Gold Souk People from all over the Middle East and the world flock to Arabia's largest gold market, where the precious metal is still sold by weight in the traditional manner. Don't expect a bargain: this is serious business. But if you're after beautifully crafted gold jewellery, with or without gems added, this is the place to come.

ⓐ Sikkat Al-Khali Street

Old Souk (Spice Souk) Few places in Dubai can make you swoon from the heady aroma of fruits and spices – in this market ginger, lemons, cinnamon and cumin all mingle and pervade the air. There are also the obligatory rug merchants, of course, and other stalls selling smaller souvenirs.

ⓐ 67 Street

Perfume Souk Located at the eastern end of the Gold Souk is another blast to the nasal senses. A huge array of European and Arabic perfumes (*attar*) are on sale here – just be aware that Western designer names may be clever copies. They might smell original on first whiff, but will quickly deteriorate. If you want a bit more spice to your aroma, opt for the Arabic versions, but apply with caution – their oil bases can stain clothes.

Sikkat Al-Khali Street

Textile Souk Textiles are probably the best and most popular souvenirs of a trip to the Middle East and you'll find whatever you're looking for here – silks, cotton, lace, wool and chiffon are all spun into wonderful designs and the prices are rock bottom compared with those at designated tourist shops.

Dubai Old Souk and Al-Faheidi Road

CULTURE

While you may not find the Tate Gallery or the Louvre in Dubai, there are a number of galleries here that exhibit art and traditional Arabic artifacts. To be honest, Western cultural experiences are not of significant importance here – don't expect to find many theatre or dance companies, or a resident orchestra. Instead immerse yourself in the Arabian opportunities at hand.

That being said, some classic culture opportunities do exist in Dubai. The Dubai Art Society was established in 1976 but only became popular when it reinvented itself in 1980 by moving to newer premises and, later, in the mid-1980s, renaming itself as the **Dubai International Arts Centre** (see page 108). Today, it is prominent in the thriving local art scene.

Ⓐ Street 75b, Villa No 27, Jumeirah Beach Road Ⓣ 4 344 4398
Ⓦ www.artdubai.com Ⓛ 08.30–17.00 Sat–Wed, 08.30–16.00 Thur

◓ *Rising high: Dubai port skyline*

Sultan Bin Ali Al-Owais Cultural Foundation

Arabia has a long and rich literary tradition, much of it originally derived by storytelling around a desert camp fire among tribal members. This foundation is dedicated to preserving this heritage – there are some 40,000 titles of Arabic literature, poetry, short stories, plays and other works stored here. The library is open to visitors but books may not be removed from the building. The foundation also hosts frequent cultural events including films and art exhibitions.

ⓐ Al-Rigga Road ⓣ 4 224 3111 ⓦ www.alowaisnet.org ⓛ 09.00–13.00 & 17.00–20.00

RETAIL THERAPY

Al-Bustan Centre In a city dominated by shopping malls, one can seem very much like another, but if you've got kids in tow head to Al-Bustan. Fantasy Kingdom is a children's paradise of funfair rides, including a pirate ship, and other attractions such as bumper cars and arcade games. ⓐ Al-Nahda Road ⓣ 4 263 0000 ⓦ www.al-bustan.com ⓛ 10.00–22.00 Sat–Thur, 16.00–22.00 Fri

Al-Ghurair Centre Although it is one of the oldest malls in Dubai, a recent renovation has ensured that it isn't showing its age. You'll find more than 400 stores here including wonderful textile and jewellery shops, as well as supermarkets, audio and video entertainment, perfumes, electronics, appliances, luggage and the largest bookstore in Dubai. If you need some refreshment, you will find fast-food outlets and ice-cream parlours located in various parts of the complex. ⓐ Al-Rigga Road ⓣ 4 222 5222 ⓦ www.alghuraircity.com ⓛ 10.00–24.00, closed Fri mornings

Al-Mulla Plaza At the Al-Mulla Plaza, there's always a market that offers clothes and other goodies at amazing discounts. This is where you are likely to discover those interesting odds and ends that you simply cannot find at malls that offer only exclusive leading brand names. Very popular with locals. ⓐ Dubai-Sharjah highway ⓣ 4 298 8999 ⓞ 10.00–13.00 & 16.30–22.30 Sat–Thur, 16.30–23.00 Fri

Deira City Centre Mall The main attractions here are Carrefour (formerly Continent), a French-style hypermarket with discounted goods, and IKEA, the well-known Swedish furniture store. The rest of the two-storey complex includes shops selling furnishings, clothing, cosmetics, perfumes and shoes. ⓐ At the junction of the Al-Garhoud Bridge Road near the Dubai Creek Golf & Yacht Club, by the Dnata intersection ⓣ 4 295 1010 ⓦ www.deiracitycentre.com ⓞ 10.00–22.00 Sat–Tues, 10.00–24.00 Wed–Fri

RECREATION & RELAXATION

Al-Badia Golf Resort The Al-Badia Golf Resort is one of the components of the Dubai Festival City development (see page 113 and map page 59). This is a par-72 championship golf course suitable for all handicaps. ⓐ Al-Rebat Street, Ras Al-Khor ⓣ 4 285 5772 ⓦ www.albadiagolfresort.com

Dubai Creek Golf & Yacht Club Almost within the heart of the city, lying along the banks of the Dubai Creek, is this championship standard golf course. The complex also includes a marina and the distinctive clubhouse that is a Dubai landmark. ⓐ Dubai Creek ⓣ 4 295 6000 ⓦ www.dubaigolf.com

Dubai Tennis Stadium This facility is home not only to the Dubai Tennis Championship, which attracts the world's top players, but also hosts live concerts and boxing matches in the 5,000-seat stadium. ⓐ Al-Garhoud ⓣ 4 216 6444 ⓦ www.dubaitennischampionships.com

TAKING A BREAK

If you have a craving for fast food you won't lack for calories in Dubai. All the major chains from Harry Ramsden's fish and chips to Dunkin'Donuts are represented. You'll even find a number of Starbucks' ready to satisfy your caffeine needs. Many of the hotels also have coffee lounges or restaurants serving cakes, sandwiches and other snacks.

Biggles Bar & Restaurant £ ❶ Dubai's legendary English pub brings a little bit of Blighty to the desert, and military enthusiasts will also enjoy the décor of World War II flying paraphernalia. The Friday brunch includes the use of the swimming pool.
ⓐ Millennium Airport Hotel, Al-Gharoud Road ⓣ 4 282 3464
ⓛ 12.00–01.30

The Terrace £ ❷ The lavish buffet is a highlight of the Friday brunch experience that is such a tradition in Dubai – the equivalent of a British Sunday lunch. The rest of the week, breakfast, lunch, afternoon tea and dinner are served. Another highlight here is the theme nights. ⓐ Sheraton Deira Hotel & Towers, Al-Mateena Street
ⓣ 4 268 8888 ⓛ 06.30–23.00

The Glasshouse ££–£££ ❸   A modern and stylish brasserie overlooking the Creek. Friday's brunch features complimentary beer. ⓐ Hilton Dubai Creek, Beniyas Road ⓣ 4 227 1111 ⓛ 06.30–23.00

Spice Island ££–£££ ❹   One of Dubai's most popular international restaurants offering everything from Mexican to Korean, Italian to Indian. Excellent Friday brunch. ⓐ Renaissance Dubai, Salah Al-Din Road ⓣ 4 262 5555 ⓛ 07.00–23.30

AFTER DARK

A night out in Dubai, if alcohol is required, will mean an evening of hopping from one hotel to another.

Restaurants

Al-Fardous £–££ ❺   If you like your Arabic music at eardrum-bursting levels, look no further. Traditional, if somewhat uninspiring, food. ⓐ Sheraton Deira Hotel & Towers, Al-Mateena Street ⓣ 4 268 8888 ⓛ 20.00–03.00

Al-Diwan ££ ❻   Head to Al-Diwan for a true taste of Arabian and Lebanese food, where you'll find *mezze* dishes and *sheesha* on the menu. Live entertainment features an Arabic singer, Lebanese band and belly dancers. ⓐ Metropolitan Palace Hotel, Al-Maktoum Road ⓣ 4 227 0000 ⓦ www.methotels.com/metpalace ⓛ 19.30–03.00

● *Middle Eastern delicacies to tempt the palate*

Harry's Place – Bar & Restaurant ££–£££ ❼ Well-known establishment for its theme nights and resident DJ. There's also a pool and darts room available. ⓐ Renaissance Dubai, Salah Al-Din Road ❶ 4 262 5555 ⏱ 12.00–02.00

Up On The Tenth ££–£££ ❽ The best jazz bar in the city, complete with a great view of the Creek. The jazz is live and the cocktails are large. ⓐ InterContinental Dubai, Beniyas Road ❶ 4 205 7333 ⏱ 19.00–03.00

Cinemas
CineStar A mall-based multiscreen theatre whose programme features all the latest Hollywood blockbusters as well as the most recent offerings from Bollywood. ⓐ Deira City Centre, Al-Ittihad Road ❶ 4 294 9000 ⓦ www.cinestarcinemas.com

Grand Cinecity Located in the Al-Ghurair mall, this multiplex screens both English and Hindi movies. ⓐ Al-Ghurair Retail Centre, Al-Rigga Road ❶ 4 228 9898

DAY-TO-DAY ETIQUETTE IN DUBAI

Dubai may seem all modern and brash, but Arabs take certain rules of etiquette very seriously. If you want to avoid appearing impolite, follow a few social rules and you'll keep a smile on the faces of your local hosts.

- Do not blow your nose or clear your throat loudly in public. If you have a cold, retreat to the bathroom for any serious sinus clearing.

- Do not sit with your back to other people.

- Do not point the soles of your feet at people, whether or not you are wearing shoes.

- Do not laugh or talk too loudly. A polite chuckle and a moderate tone of voice is the order of the day.

- Do not eat while standing or walking about. Especially, do not eat while walking in the street. This goes for slurping from your water bottle, too.

- Always use your right hand for eating, or for handing anything to anyone, or receiving.

- Do not offer your hand to a woman, unless she offers it to you first.

Bur Dubai

Bur Dubai was once a residential area housing the city's elite.
Nowadays it is a bustling commercial and shopping district.

SIGHTS & ATTRACTIONS

Al-Boom Tourist Village

By day this area is likely to have little appeal to general visitors,
despite its name. It serves as a conference centre for the many
business travellers that come to the city all year round. At night,
however, this is the place to board a traditional dhow for a gentle
cruise tour of the Creek and to take in the sights on the waterfront.
Boats depart nightly at 20.30.

ⓐ Al-Qataiyat Road ⓣ 4 324 3000 ⓛ 09.00–01.00

Bastakiya

Walking around the old Bastakiya district on the eastern side of town
beside the Creek is like stepping into a time warp. This is 'Old Dubai',
an area of narrow alleyways and courtyards and houses that, prior to
the invention of air conditioning, were cooled by wind towers.

The traditional Arabian architecture that can be seen in
Al-Bastakiya today dates back to the early 1900s, and the masonry,
particularly to the east of Al-Fahidi Fort, is so impressive that
the area has been preserved as a heritage area.

ⓐ East of Dubai Souk on Al-Fahidi Street

Children's City

Children love nothing more than interactive games as a means of
education, and they have their fill here – numerous exhibits will

have them pushing buttons and pulling handles to learn about the human body, space travel, the world and much, much more.

ⓐ Creekside Park ⓣ 4 334 0808 ⓦ www.childrencity.ae

ⓛ 09.00–20.30 Sat–Thur, 15.00–20.30 Fri; admission charge

Creekside Park

This beautiful green park, on the west shore of the Creek, is an irrigation wonder in the midst of this desert landscape. This vast area, particularly popular with local families at the weekend, has a variety of facilities including a full-size golf course and a children's games area. The park also has plenty of picnic opportunities and a large amphitheatre that can accommodate 5,000 people for concerts and dramatic events.

ⓐ Between Al-Maktoum and Al-Garhoud bridges ⓛ 08.00–21.30; women and children only Wed

Diwan

The Dubai government, known as the Diwan, is housed within this modern and impressive building graced by wind towers, sculptures and a black cast-iron fence, as are the offices of the current ruler of Dubai, Sheikh Al-Maktoum. The building is not open to the public.

ⓐ Opposite Dubai Museum

Dubai Museum

The Dubai Museum is housed in the 19th-century Al-Fahidi Fort, built of coral and lime originally to defend the city in case of invasion by neighbouring tribes. Today the museum is the city's most important collection of relics and memorabilia from its

◀ *Old Dubai: the Bastakiya quarter*

centuries-old history. Documents, manuscripts, archaeological finds, musical instruments and a natural history section exploring the wildlife of the desert are among the exhibits. For nostalgia buffs there's also a replica of a traditional Arab house from the 1950s.
ⓐ Al-Fahidi Fort, Al-Fahidi Road ❶ 4 393 7151 ❶ 08.00–22.00 Sat–Thur, 08.00–11.00 & 16.00–22.00 Fri; 09.00–24.00 (Ramadan); admission charge

Grand Mosque
One of Dubai's major landmarks is the Grand Mosque, built in the 1990s and recognisable from all around by its soaring minaret. Despite its modern construction, the architects emulated the former building (demolished in 1960) and used pale walls and wooden shutters to allow it to blend seamlessly with its surroundings. Non-Muslims will have to appreciate its beauty from the outside, however (only practising Muslims are allowed to enter), which is a shame because they will miss the beautiful and intricate blue tiling that lines the interior walls.
ⓐ Al-Mussalla Road (near Diwan) ❶ 24 hours; admission free but non-Muslims are not permitted to enter

Heritage & Diving Village
Located close to the Creek mouth, this re-creation of a traditional village allows visitors to explore the architectural, cultural and maritime heritage of the Emirate. Here you can learn about the pearl diving industry (see opposite) and Bedouin tribal life and experience the atmosphere of a traditional souk. Potters and weavers also create and display their wares, all made in the time-honoured way. Children in particular will enjoy the experience of a camel ride. Just don't expect to experience any of this on your own – the place is always crowded.

🅐 The mouth of the Creek, Al-Shindagha 📞 4 393 7151
🕐 08.00–22.00 Sat–Thur, 08.00–11.00 & 16.00–22.00 Fri;
09.00–12.00 Mon–Sat, closed Sun (Ramadan)

PRECIOUS PEARLS

The tradition of pearling can trace its roots far back into Middle Eastern history, to at least six or seven thousand years ago, and it played a significant role in the economy of the region for centuries. Pearl oysters thrive in the shallow bank areas of the Arabian Gulf and, for about four months of each year, diving for these precious gems was an additional income for Bedouin tribes who made their living from farming the land for the rest of the year.

In the late 16th century, Europeans began to develop an interest in pearls as a precious commodity, and for almost 400 years the pearling industry became an important part of the overall economic scheme of the entire Emirate region.

The early 20th century, however, brought two events that were devastating for pearling. The first was the Japanese development of cultured pearls, which severely undermined the demand for traditional pearls. The second was the worldwide Great Depression of the 1930s, which meant a lack of surplus cash to spend on luxuries and proved the final nail in the coffin for this industry. This created great hardship in the region, as a single pearling vessel could employ up to 20 men working as divers, haulers, cooks and apprentices.

It would not be until the discovery of oil in the 1960s that the Emirate region of the Arabian Peninsula began to recover from severe economic problems.

Narish Khyma

Not far from the Dubai Museum, boat-lovers will find much to interest them in this collection of traditional vessels. Among the exhibits is a replica of an *abra* – the ferry boat still used for transporting passengers across Dubai's Creek. ⓐ Near Dubai Museum

Sheikh Saeed Al-Maktoum House

This late 19th-century house, built for the then ruler of Dubai, Sheikh Saeed, is one of the best places in the city to appreciate the traditional Arabian architecture of the ruling classes. Courtyards, verandahs, wind towers and intricate carving are all features that have earned it heritage status. Today there is a museum inside dedicated to the history of Dubai. It's particularly beautiful when floodlit at night.
ⓐ Al-Shindagha Road ⏰ 07.30–21.30 Sat–Thur, 15.00–21.30 Fri; admission charge

Wonderland Theme & Water Park

A fairly standard water park, with slides, wave pools and other watery fun – great for a hot day. For land lovers there is also plenty on hand to entertain, including arcade games, slot machines, bumper car and power karts. Arabic bands perform on Wednesday, Thursday and Friday nights.
ⓐ Near Creekside Park ☎ 4 324 1222 ⏰ 14.00–20.00 Mon–Sat, women only Wed, closed Sun; admission charge

---

● *Bur Dubai mosque*

CULTURE

Majlis Gallery

The Majlis Gallery opened in 1989 as a community project to showcase local arts and artisans, housed in a traditional building that was one of the first to be restored in the Bastakiya area. The gallery hosts about ten annual exhibitions featuring the work of both local and international artists.

🅐 Al-Fahidi Street, Bastakiya 🕾 4 353 6233 🕑 09.30–13.30 & 16.30–20.00 Sat–Thur, closed Fri

XVA Gallery

The XVA Gallery is a curious combination of guesthouse and art gallery. Four exhibition rooms exhibit contemporary paints, sculptures and 'installations'. It is worth a visit simply to spend some time in the serene courtyard setting with its traditional wind-tower architecture.

🅐 Bastakiya, behind Majlis Gallery 🕾 4 353 5383 🕑 09.30–20.00 Sat–Thur, closed Fri

RETAIL THERAPY

Bur Jurman Centre Three levels of boutiques and shops featuring international designer names such as Christian Dior, Max Mara, Kenzo and Polo Ralph Lauren. Once you've shopped till you've almost dropped, head to the food court on the top level where there's the option of a snack, a drink or a full-scale sit-down meal.

🅐 Trade Centre Road 🕾 4 352 0222 🕑 10.00–22.00 Sat–Thur, 13.00–22.00 Fri

Electronics Souk Dubai has the cheapest prices on electronics in all of the UAE, but if you're buying in the souk, take a few precautions. Check price comparisons before buying and always check that the item actually works before leaving the shop. ⓐ Al-Sabkha Road & Al-Maktoum Hospital Road ⓛ 07.00–12.00 & 17.00–19.00 Sat–Thur, 17.00–19.00 Fri

TAKING A BREAK

Dôme £ ❶   Located in the Bur Jurman Centre, this is a relaxed coffee shop owned by an Australian company. The food ranges from pizzas to cakes and there are tables outside for alfresco eating. ⓐ Bur Jurman Centre ⓣ 4 355 6004 ⓛ 07.30–01.30 daily

XVA Gallery £ ❷   The vegetarian delights of this little restaurant will have you returning again and again. ⓐ Bastakiya, behind Majlis Gallery ⓣ 4 353 5383 ⓛ 09.30–20.00 Sat–Thur, closed Fri

Basta Art Café £–££ ❸   When the heat crashes in on you, retreat to the Basta Art Café for a soothing lemon-mint cocktail, a traditional drink of old Dubai. This peaceful, shady courtyard setting is a local favourite. Popular menu items include jacket potatoes, salads, wraps and sandwiches. ⓐ Al-Fahidi Road near Al-Musallah roundabout ⓣ 4 353 5701 ⓛ 10.00–20.00 Sat–Thur, closed Fri

AFTER DARK

Fatafeet £ ❹   Tempting, traditional Middle Eastern food is the order of the day at Fatafeet. The *mezze*, falafel, kebabs and houmous are delicious and the view at sunset is an added bonus.

🅐 Al-Seef Road, near the British Embassy 🕽 4 397 9222
🕒 10.30–24.00

Local House £ 🟨 If you want to eat like a local, cross-legged in a *majlis* setting, or at an outside table, Local House is a truly authentic Dubaian experience. A good choice of meal is the spicy chicken. 🅐 Al-Fahidi Street, Bastakiya 🕽 4 353 9997 🕒 10.00–23.00 Sat–Thur, 13.00–22.00 Fri

Kwality ££ 🟨 If you have a large appetite head to Kwality – the portions are vast while the prices remain reasonable. If you are a single woman travelling alone, ask for a seat upstairs in the family section. This is a very popular restaurant so be sure to book in advance for weekends or holidays. 🅐 Opposite Ascot Hotel Dubai, Khalid Bin Al-Waleed Road 🕽 4 393 6563 🕒 13.00–14.45 & 20.00–23.45

Rock Bottoms ££ 🟨 Night owls will welcome the lively atmosphere and late opening hours of Rock Bottoms. This Dubai stalwart is extremely popular and known for its great music and live bands. The bar food is limited but they do make a good *shawarma* (kebab) to keep the munchies at bay. 🅐 Regent Palace Hotel, World Trade Centre Road 🕽 4 396 3888 🕒 07.00–03.00

Bateaux Dubai £££ 🟨 This beautiful, glass-enclosed cruise ship serves up gourmet meals; you can enjoy the sights of the Creek while you eat. 🅐 Al-Seef Road, near the British Embassy 🕽 4 399 4994 🕒 Public cruises available 12.30–15.00 Wed & Thur, 20.30–23.00 Mon, Wed, Thur & Fri

🔘 *The stunning Emirates Towers*

Sheikh Zayed Road & Oud Metha

Dubai's image as a city of glistening high-rises and skyscrapers owes much to the dramatic architecture along Sheikh Zayed Road. Here, shopping malls, hotels and apartment and office buildings all vie for attention, looming over the landscape in striking modernity. It's all a far cry from traditional Arab alleyways and desert living. If you're walking around this part of town, however, do have your road awareness skills on full alert – the eight-lane highway is more of a racing track than a road to local drivers. If you're thinking of driving yourself, keep your wits about you.

The Oud Metha district lies just to the east of the busy Sheikh Zayed area. In contrast to all the bustle and noise, this is an area dedicated to leisure activities such as ice skating, cable-car rides, theme parks and, of course, shopping.

SIGHTS & ATTRACTIONS

Al-Nasr Leisureland

You might not associate winter sports with Dubai, but think again. Ski Dubai has been an unprecedented success (see pages 37 & 54) and here at Al-Nasr is one of two ice rinks in the city that always seem to draw plenty of punters. Skates can be hired on site. If you'd rather stick to less slippery ground, there's a bowling alley and tennis and squash courts. There's also a pool, but if you want to mess about on slides and enjoy other water park features, the Wonderland Theme Park (see page 86) is a better bet.

ⓐ Off Oud Metha ⓣ 4 337 1234 ⓦ www.alnasrll.com ⓛ 09.00–24.00; admission charge

Architecture of Sheikh Zayed Road

The overall attraction of Sheikh Zayed Road is its modern architecture that has lent Dubai its reputation for wealth and glamour. The Fairmont Hotel, Dusit Dubai, the Emirates Towers and the Dubai World Trade Centre are just a few of the buildings that will have you craning your neck in awe and wondering at the skills of the architects and construction workers involved.

Gold & Diamond Park & Museum

Arabic jewellery is renowned the world over for its intricacy and style. This museum offers guided tours of a real working jewellery factory allowing visitors to see the pieces being made and the skills and artistry involved. There are also opportunities to buy and, unusually for Dubai, because there are few shops in the area, the craftsmen are willing to bargain.

🅐 Near interchange No 4, Sheikh Zayed Road 🅣 4 347 7788

🕒 10.00–22.00 Sat–Thur, 16.00–22.00 Fri

Safa Park

Families flock to Safa Park, on the Dubai–Abu Dhabi highway, particularly at weekends. The entire area, covering more than 60 hectares (148 acres), is given over to leisure and entertainment, including volleyball, basketball and tennis areas, an athletics track and a children's maze and play area. There are also designated barbecue areas ideal for rustling up your own kebab. As is common in Arabian society, there is also an area entirely reserved for women and children. If the outside temperature is

◀ *The maze at Safa Park*

overbearing, however, don't despair – an indoor air-conditioned centre offers all the usual noisy arcade games.

ⓐ Sheikh Zayed Road ❶ 4 349 2111

ⓦ www.vgn.dm.gov.ae/DMEGOV/dm-pasafa-info

🕒 08.00–23.00, women and children only Tues

CULTURE

The Courtyard

If you're interested in art and architecture, this is the place to come – all aspects of building design are explored and examined here and blended into a fascinating whole. There are also craftspeople and artisans at work, so you can pick up a beautifully designed souvenir.

ⓐ Near Interchange No 4, Sheikh Zayed Road

Dubai Community Theatre & Arts Centre

(Due to open at the end of 2006.) The premier arts facility in the city includes a theatre with a capacity for more than 500 audience members, art galleries and classrooms where lessons in photography, painting and sculpture are on offer.

ⓐ Mall of the Emirates, Sheikh Zayed Road ❶ 4 409 9000

ⓦ www.malloftheemirates.com

RETAIL THERAPY

Emirates Towers Shopping Boulevard Another extremely smart designer option with the great names of European design – Gucci, Giorgio Armani and Yves Saint Laurent – bringing their

---

▶ *Track down that designer outfit at Emirates Towers*

creations to the desert. ⓐ Emirates Towers ⓣ 4 318 8999
ⓦ www.jumeirahemiratestowers.com ⓛ 10.00–22.00 Sat–Thur,
16.00–22.00 Fri

Ibn Battuta Mall Historically themed mall based on the global
travels of the 14th-century Arabian explorer, Ibn Battuta. Six
designated areas are all themed on the places he visited, including
an Andalusian Court, a North African Court, an Egyptian Court,
an Indian Court and a Chinese Court, with goods on offer in each
reflecting those destinations. ⓐ Sheikh Zayed Road ⓣ 4 362 1900
ⓦ www.ibnbattutamall.com ⓛ 10.00–22.00 Sat–Tues, 10.00–24.00
Wed–Fri

Lamcy Plaza Just a stone's throw away from Wafi City you'll find this
five-storey mall has a Tower of London theme as its basis. This is one
of the best malls for bargains, particularly during Eid (the festival
that follows Ramadan). An excellent choice if you are feeling
peckish, the food courts serve a full range of international cuisine.
ⓐ Al-Karama ⓣ 4 335 9999 ⓦ www.lamcyplaza.com
ⓛ 09.00–22.00 Sat–Tues, 09.00–22.30 Wed–Fri

Mall of the Emirates Yet another extravaganza of shopping, as well
as a hotel (the Kempinksi), cinemas and a family entertainment
section including indoor roller coasters. The mall is also home to one
of Dubai's newest attractions, Ski Dubai (see pages 37 & 54).
ⓐ Sheikh Zayed Road ⓣ 4 409 9000 ⓦ www.malloftheemirates.com
ⓛ 10.00–24.00 Wed–Fri, 10.00–22.00 Sat–Tues

◖ *Sheikh Zayed Road is dominated by high-rises*

Oasis Centre Furniture, shoes, baby clothes and a hypermarket are just some of the offerings of the Oasis Centre. There's also Fun City, an entertainment centre that is sure to keep kids amused if they're bored of trawling around shops. ⓐ Sheikh Zayed Road ❶ 4 339 5111 Ⓦ www.landmarkgroupco.com ❶ 10.00–22.00 Sat–Thur, 14.00–22.00 Fri

Wafi City Mall Wafi in Arabic translates as 'to satisfy everything you want' and here it certainly lives up to its name. The mall has an elegant Egyptian theme to its design, complete with two giant sphinxes flanking the entrance, but inside the influence is definitely European, with the very best of designer offerings, dripping in luxury. For shoppers with children there's an added advantage – you can park your kids in the entertainment arcades to keep them amused while you shop. ⓐ Al-Garhood Road ❶ 4 324 4555 Ⓦ waficity.com/waficitymall/index.htm ❶ 10.00–22.00 Sat–Thur, 16.30–22.00 Fri

TAKING A BREAK

In the Sheikh Zayed/Oud Metha area, the malls are your best bet for finding a quick and simple meal. All of the malls mentioned above feature either a food court or a wide selection of restaurants and fast-food outlets, including McDonald's, Burger King and KFC.

AFTER DARK

The Agency ££ ❶ A very smart wine bar with a sophisticated atmosphere. With more than 50 wines on the menu, grape lovers will be in their element here. The food served is really an accompaniment to the wine rather than a full meal, with dishes such as pâté, plates of cheese and fondues. Located on the lower level of the shopping boulevard of the Emirates Towers. ⓐ Emirates Towers ⓣ 4 319 8785 ⓛ 12.30–01.00 Sat–Thur, 15.00–01.00 Fri

Harry Ghatos Karaoke Bar ££ ❷ The number one karaoke bar in Dubai, complete with singing hostesses and light Japanese fare. There are also monthly singing competitions – but note that you need to book in advance if you want to be a contender.
ⓐ Emirates Towers ⓣ 4 319 8786 ⓛ 22.00–03.00

● *Dubai's wide, open boulevards*

Jumeirah & Satwa

This elegant stretch of coastline just west of the city centre is home to an astonishing array of shopping emporiums, luxurious hotels and some of the most extraordinary buildings to be found in the entire Middle East. Most famous of all is the Burj Al Arab hotel (see page 46), its construction resembling a billowing sail, which is now as much of a landmark in Dubai as the Eiffel Tower is in Paris or the Opera House in Sydney. However, with even more fantastical buildings beginning to blossom, Dubai may soon have difficulty determining just which landmark will fix the city in the mind of the traveller.

SIGHTS & ATTRACTIONS

Dubai Zoo

Located opposite Jumeirah Beach, the zoo is an oasis, home to more than 240 species of animals. It is just one more example of how this area never does anything by half measures. Habitats have been recreated to be as close as possible to the native environment for animals such as gorillas, hyenas, pumas, lions, jaguars, chimpanzees and giraffes, as well as a number of endangered species including Bengal tigers and Arabian wolves. Avian life is made up from the very small to the very large, including ostriches, while there's also a colourful collection of parrots from around the world. A reptile house will appeal to those who like their creatures scaly and slithery.

ⓐ Jumeirah Road ⓣ 4 344 0462 ⓛ 10.00–17.30 Wed–Mon, closed Tues

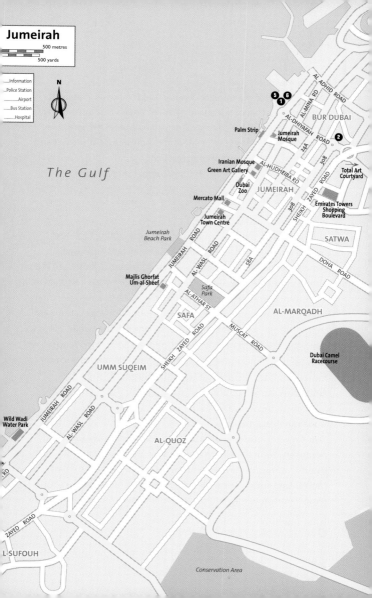

Jumeirah

500 metres
500 yards

- ....Information
- ....Police Station
- ....Airport
- ....Bus Station
- ....Hospital

N

The Gulf

AL ADHID ROAD

AL MINA RD

BUR DUBAI

AL-DHIYAFAH

❺ ❻
❶

Palm Strip

Jumeirah
Mosque

24A

❷

Iranian Mosque
Green Art Gallery

AL-HUDHEIBA RD

SHEIKH ZAYED ROAD

308

Total Art
Courtyard

Dubai
Zoo

JUMEIRAH

Mercato Mall

308

Emirates Towers
Shopping
Boulevard

Jumeirah
Town Centre

SATWA

Jumeirah
Beach Park

JUMEIRAH ROAD

AL WASL ROAD

38A

DOHA ROAD

Majlis Ghorfat
Um-al-Sheef

Safa
Park

AL ATHAR ST

AL-MARQADH

SAFA

MUSCAT ROAD

SHEIKH ZAYED ROAD

Dubai Camel
Racecourse

UMM SUQEIM

Wild Wadi
Water Park

JUMEIRAH ROAD

AL WASL ROAD

AL-QUOZ

ZAYED ROAD

L-SUFOUH

Conservation Area

Iranian Mosque

The highlight of the Iranian Mosque and the hospital opposite are the traditional Persian blue and green mosaics on the building façades. It also makes for a striking photo when shot with the backdrop of the Emirates Towers – a classic image of the old and new that so often juxtaposes in this city.

ⓐ Al-Wasl Road ⏺ 24 hours ❶ entrance to non-Muslims is forbidden

Jumeirah Archaeological Site

Although you'd barely know it from the surrounding high-rise shopping malls, this is one of the most important and largest archaeological sites in the region, with finds even dating from the pre-Islamic era. Once a trading post on the route between Iraq and Oman, remains of houses – including a governor's palace, a souk and many other significant buildings – have been found and excavations are ongoing. Because of that, the site is not open to the public, but you can watch the archaeologists in action from behind the fence as well as see some of the uncovered items, including ceramics and coins, in the museum at the Heritage & Diving Village (see page 84).

ⓐ Between Jumeirah and Al-Wasl Roads ⏺ 07.30–14.00

Jumeirah Beach Park

This park is a local favourite for all ages, not only because of its advantageous location but the wide variety of activities it offers, including volleyball courts and a children's playground. There are special areas designated for picnics, and the beautiful surroundings provide for a relaxing and enjoyable open-air experience. The park

⏵ *East meets West in architectural form*

also has an amphitheatre that offers dramatic and musical entertainment.

 Jumeirah Road 4 349 2555
 vgn.dm.gov.ae/DMEGOV/dm-park-jumeirah 08.00–23.00, women & children only Sat & Sun

Jumeirah Mosque

One of the largest and most beautiful mosques in the city, Jumeirah Mosque is a spectacular example of modern Islamic skill at re-creating traditional medieval styles. The mosque is particularly attractive at night when floodlights enhance the domes and minarets.

 Jumeirah Road 24 hours, access to non-Muslims through organised tours only

Majlis Ghorfat Um-al-Sheef

This restored traditional house, built of coral and lime, was once the place where Sheikh Rashid bin Saeed Al-Maktoum would hold open debates and listen to the complaints, grievances and ideas of his people. The *majlis* (meeting room) also provided a retreat from the intense heat of the day. Today a beautiful garden of date palms and fig trees has been added to the house and makes for a wonderful refreshment spot in the café, soothed by the gentle trickling water of the fountain.

 Jumeirah Road 4 394 6343 08.30–13.30 & 15.30–20.30 Sat–Thur, 15.30–20.30 Fri

 The beautiful Jumeirah Mosque

CULTURE

Dubai International Arts Centre
Look out for special events and exhibitions in a range of media.
ⓐ Beach Road ① 4 344 4398 ⓦ www.artdubai.com ⏰ 08.30–18.30
Sat–Wed, 08.30–15.30 Thur

Green Art Gallery
The works displayed here are mostly of international artists.
However, you will find a good selection of art that is largely
influenced by Islam and its culture.
ⓐ 51 Street, behind the Dubai Zoo ① 4 344 9888
ⓦ www.gagallery.com ⏰ 09.30–13.30 & 16.30–20.30 Sat–Thur

Total Art Courtyard
Everything the name implies. This courtyard gallery displays
paintings, calligraphy, sculpture and miniature Persian carpets.
ⓐ Sheikh Zayed Road ① 4 347 5050 ⓦ www.courtyard-uae.com

RETAIL THERAPY

Jumeirah Town Centre The Town Centre of Jumeirah emulates just
that – the whole urban experience. Aside from shopping you can
take a class in pottery in **Ceramiques**, have your hair or nails done,
post a letter and then relax in the courtyard area. ⓐ Jumeirah Road
① 4 344 4161 ⓦ www.towncentrejumeirah.com

Mercato Mall This Renaissance-themed mall is among the newer
additions to Dubai's shopping scene and certainly adds a bit of
colour to the Jumeirah Road. You'll find all the usual here, such as

designer brands, shoe shops, cosmetics, furniture, as well as a supermarket and a Virgin Megastore. There's also a multiplex cinema on site and an ever useful children's play area to keep the little ones amused. ⓐ Jumeirah Road ⓣ 4 344 0111 ⓦ www.mercatoshoppingmall.com

Palm Strip This is the place to come if you've got teenagers in tow. The emphasis is definitely on the young and trendy market, with good-value chainstores such as Mango, Beyond the Beach, and Young Designers Emporium. There are also music stores and plenty of food outlets. ⓐ Jumeirah Road ⓣ 4 224 9222

🔺 *Burj Al-Arab from Wild Wadi Water Park*

RECREATION & RELAXATION

Wild Wadi Water Park

Dubai's largest water park takes its theme from Sinbad the Sailor and features a wide variety of adrenaline-pumping rides that all interconnect for one long, exhilarating experience. If you prefer your water with a little less splash, there are quieter rides and gentle wave pools. If you have young children, there's also the advantage of trained lifeguards watching over the proceedings. You can rent towels and lockers and there are plenty of places for a snack should all the aquatic hurtling make you peckish.

ⓐ Jumeirah Beach ⓣ 4 348 4444 ⓛ 11.00–19.00 Sat–Tues, 11.00–21.00 Wed–Fri; admission charge

◙ Take a break at a Jumeirah hotel

TAKING A BREAK

The best places for taking a break in the Jumeirah/Satwa area are the hotels and shopping malls. Poolside eateries are popular and the food courts of the malls are extensive.

AFTER DARK

The Alamo £ ❶ Rough and ready is the only way to describe the Alamo. Really a guy place, with hearty Tex Mex food and sports screenings, but they do cater for women with free champagne on Sundays, Tuesdays and Thursdays. ⓐ Dubai Marine Beach Resort & Spa, Jumeirah Road ❶ 4 346 1111 ⓦ www.dxbmarine.com

Aussie Legends £ ❷ A favourite of the Aussie expats, this lively bar serves simple but tasty snacks and is renowned for its friendly if slightly raucous atmosphere. Monday night is traditionally Quiz Night, while Thursday has the Happy Hour (13.00–19.00). ⓐ Rydges Plaza, Al-Dhiyafah Road, Satwa Roundabout ❶ 4 398 2222 ⓦ www.rydges.com/dubai

Kasbar ££ ❸ If you've ever longed to frequent a 1950s-style club lounge, head for Kasbar. Tables hug the dance floor, candles create a romantic note and the upstairs balcony is a perfect place to perch and watch the action on the floor below. Perenially popular with a smart, young crowd. ⓐ Royal Mirage Hotel, Jumeirah Road ❶ 4 399 9999 ⓦ www.oneandonlyresorts.com/flash.html

Rooftop Lounge & Terrace ££–£££ ❹ Lie back on a cushion-covered banquette with Persian rugs at your feet, feel the glow of Moroccan

lamps and candles and immerse yourself in the sumptuousness of
this truly Arabian atmosphere. A wonderful place to rekindle a
romance while watching the sun set over the sea.
ⓐ The One&Only Royal Mirage, Jumeirah Road ⓣ 4 399 9999
ⓦ www.oneandonlyresorts.com

Sho Cho's ££–£££ ❺ Minimalism is the key note in this high-tech,
cutting-edge sushi bar, decorated with comfy white leather
armchairs all lit under a pale blue glow. The aquariums built into
the walls lend the place an underwater feel.
ⓐ Dubai Marine Beach Resort & Spa, Jumeirah Road ⓣ 4 346 1111
ⓦ www.dxbmarine.com

Boudoir £££ ❻ You can imagine yourself in the heart of Paris
inside Boudoir, and you'll need to dress like a chic Parisian to feel at
home here. Bring a heavy wallet – the drinks are as expensive as
they are elegant. Definitely Dubai's place to see and be seen.
ⓐ Dubai Marine Beach Resort & Spa, Jumeirah Beach Road
ⓣ 4 345 5995 ⓦ www.myboudoir.com

Tagine £££ ❼ Very classy, very upmarket Moroccan restaurant.
Waiters dressed in traditional Moroccan garb are on hand to both
serve and entertain. A wonderfully sumptuous and romantic
experience all round. ⓐ Royal Mirage Hotel, Jumeirah Road
ⓣ 4 399 9999 ⓦ www.oneandonlyresorts.com/flash.html

Dubai's coming attractions

Burj Dubai
Dubai is a city of superlatives and here's the latest one. Purportedly the largest building in the world, the Burj Dubai tower is being constructed in the downtown district. The vast space will feature luxury apartments, the Armani Hotel, a health club, a multitude of shops and restaurants and a library. Completion is expected in 2008.

Dubai Festival City
Festival City is envisioned to be an all-in-one complex incorporating housing, shopping and entertainment, and is already well under construction. The first phase, which opened in November 2005, houses retail outlets such as the largest IKEA store in the UAE. Several hotels are also under construction at this site including a Four Seasons, W Hotel and an InterContinental hotel.

Dubailand
Only the Emirates would take on the challenge of creating a Disneyworld-type theme park in the desert. Dubailand is intended to be the world's largest attraction, with different themed 'worlds' such as Desert Kingdom and Giants' World, a huge sports area, parklands, water parks, health retreats, resorts, hotels and, of course, the world's largest shopping mall. Completion is ambitiously expected for 2007.

Dubai Metro/Railway Project
This much-needed public transport system will have two lines, with phase one running from the Sharjah border to Jebel Ali, and the second from the Dubai airport to the Ghubaiba area. The driverless system should be fully operational by 2010.

Palm Islands

A continental shelf and the shallowness of the Persian Gulf make it possible for Dubai to continually expand its landmass with artificial islands, as has proved so successful with the Burj Al Arab hotel (see page 46). The Palm Islands are three new such projects, so named because they are being constructed in the shape of a palm tree, which is such an important symbol of the city. Each island will house both residential communities and holiday resorts. The Palm Jumeirah is expected to be completed in 2006, the Palm Jebel Ali in 2007 and the Palm Deira by 2012. According to some, the islands will be so large they will be visible from outer space – the only man-made structures to do so other than the Great Wall of China.

Snowdome

Following the success of Ski Dubai (see page 54), work began on this new project in February 2006. This leisure winter wonderland will have all the attractions of a snow and ice recreational park. Completion is expected in 2008.

The World Islands

Another planned collection of man-made islands take their name from the fact that they've been designed to resemble each of the world's five continents. The World will cover an area of 9 km (5½ miles) in length and 6 km (4 miles) in width, accessed by boat or plane. More luxurious hotel complexes are planned for the islands, but they will also serve as private residences. The project is so large that it will take several years – a completion date has not yet been predicted.

▶ *The Blue (Central) Souk in Sharjah*

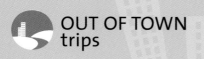

Desert delights

Desert safari

No visitor to Dubai should miss the opportunity to undertake a desert safari. Leaving the city in mid-afternoon, the tour guides drive you far out into the desert to a Bedouin-style encampment, where you'll be served a traditional meal under the stars, sleep in specially arranged tents and wake to the smell of freshly brewed coffee. After breakfast you'll head for the mountains while taking in the rugged scenery of the wadis (dry riverbeds) before returning to the city.

Hatta Rock Pools

The Hatta Rock Pools are one of the most popular weekend escapes, particularly when temperatures soar in the city. Located in the Hajar Mountains, where the climate is considerably cooler, young and old flock here to swim in the pools fed from the waterfalls cascading down this mini-canyon. Visit during the week if you want a more peaceful experience – and remember that weekend in Dubai means Thursday and Friday.

Heritage Village of Hatta

The Hatta Mountains, 115 km (71½ miles) southeast of the city, are home to a village estimated to be around 2,000 years old and therefore one of the oldest regions of the Emirate. In 2001 it was turned into a heritage village to allow visitors to trace the history and discover the mysteries of ancient Arabian life. Around 30 buildings, each differing in size, interior layout and building materials can be explored, as can two towers overlooking the village, known as the 'two stones' that were used as defence fortresses against hostile invaders.

Sand-dune skiing

It certainly isn't as glamorous as a day at Aspen or St Moritz, and your après-ski drink will definitely be a cool one. Sand-dune skiing or sand-boarding is a truly unique experience. Many tour companies offer packages that include both transportation and instruction. Expect to pay about Dh 200 to give it a try. Be sure to wear lots of sunscreen to protect you from the intense desert sun.

Wadi bashing

Wadis are dry riverbeds that follow undulating paths through rocky valleys that have been carved out by seasonal flooding. Taking a trip through these rugged landscape features is a highlight of any trip to the Arabian Peninsula.

Wadi bashing involves driving this challenging terrain in 4WD vehicles. It is recommended that you hire a driver to take charge of the wheel, who is likely to be very experienced in handling a vehicle in this landscape. It is possible to hire a 4WD and do the driving yourself, however. If this is your chosen option, keep a few tips in mind:

Tyre pressures should be only one-half to two-thirds that of normal to get the best traction in soft sand.

It can be easy to lose your way in the desert, so be sure to bring a compass and make a note of landmarks wherever possible. When renting a 4WD vehicle for your adventure, make sure you pack a spade or shovel, tow-rope, planks of wood, spare wheel car jack, and extra petrol.

Ensure you have enough food, water, sunglasses, hats, first-aid kit, toilet rolls and rubbish bags to service both you and your passengers.

Sharjah

About 20 minutes north of Dubai is the Emirate of Sharjah, the region's unofficial cultural centre. Known as the 'City of Knowledge', it is defined by its striking Arabic architecture and fine museums and renowned for its expertise in the craft of rug making. Such is its dedication to heritage sites and buildings that it was designated a cultural capital by UNESCO in 1998.

Geographically it also benefits from having two coasts – one on the Arabian Gulf and one on the Gulf of Oman – as well as oasis areas such as Al-Dhaid, which generate successful agriculture in the growing of fruit and vegetables.

Visitors to Sharjah, however, should be aware that this Emirate does not have the cosmopolitan tolerance of Dubai. Alcohol is banned everywhere, clothing must cover the body (swimsuits are not allowed) and unmarried couples will have to stay in separate rooms in hotels. It's also not that easy to get around – there is no bus service so the only option is to walk or to take a taxi. If opting for the latter, make sure you agree the fare before you get in the car: all taxis here are unmetered.

SIGHTS & ATTRACTIONS

Bait Sheikh Sultan bin Saqr Al-Qassimi
This is part of the Heritage Museum. Built by His Highness Sheikh Sultan bin Saqr Al-Qassimi in 1820, the fort preserved its official as well as public status until 1969. It has now been restored to its original 19th-century design.
ⓐ Sharjah Heritage Museum, Al-Ayubi Road ⓣ 6 569 3999
ⓦ www.shjmuseum.gov.ae/museums ⓛ 09.00–13.00 &

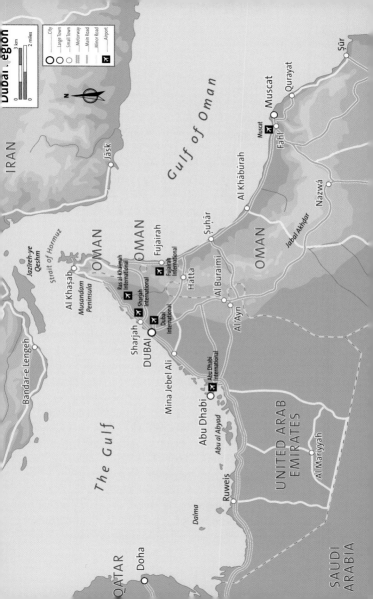

City
Large Town
Small Town
Motorway
Main Road
Minor Road
Airport

0   3 km
0   2 miles

N

IRAN

Bandar-e Lengeh

Jazīreh-ye Qeshm

Strait of Hormuz

Jāsk

The Gulf

Dalma

QATAR

Doha

Al Khaṣab

Musandam Peninsula

OMAN

OMAN

Ras al-Khaimah International

Sharjah International

Sharjah

DUBAI

Dubai International

Fujairah

Fujairah International

Gulf of Oman

Al Khābūrah

Ṣuḥār

Hatta

Al Buraimi

OMAN

Nazwā

Jabal Akhḍar

Muscat

Muscat

Fahl

Qurayat

Ṣūr

Mina Jebel Ali

Abu Dhabi

Abu Dhabi International

Abu al Abyad

UNITED ARAB EMIRATES

Al'Ayn

Ruweis

Al Mariyyah

SAUDI ARABIA

CARPET BUYING

No visit to Arabia is complete without a trip to a carpet store. There are carpet outlets in most shopping centres but, for the essential flavour of the region, a trip to a carpet souk is a must.

The whole carpet-buying process is an experience in itself. The vendors take great pride and passion in their work and will unfurl one carpet after another for you to look at while you sip on mint tea, usually starting at the lower end of the spectrum (wool on wool) then working their way up to the most expensive (silk on silk).

The most expensive and sought-after carpets are the traditional Persian ones from Iran, which are usually handmade from silk with the weaver's own signature incorporated into the design. The designs themselves are varied, and some date back generations following the traditions of local tribes. If these are out of your price range, however, don't despair. Similar carpets using lesser materials are available from India, Kashmir, Pakistan and Afghanistan. The vendor will be able to tell you the origins of each carpet and the method and materials used in their creation. If, however, you don't feel you're getting the information you require, remember to ask whether the carpet has been made by hand or by machine, whether natural or artificial dyes have been used, and how many knots there are per square inch: the greater number of knots, the better quality of carpet.

One of the best places to purchase a carpet is the Blue Souk in Sharjah, which offers the widest range of carpets at the most competitive prices, but most carpet souks will carry an assortment of both ancient and modern carpets.

16.00–20.00 Sat, Sun, Tues–Thur, 16.30–20.30 Fri, closed Mon, women & children only Wed evening; admission free

Islamic Museum

Anyone interested in Islamic culture will be fascinated by the items on display here, including scientific, literary and religious manuscripts, traditional ceramics, Islamic jewellery and other metal items, as well as ancient coins and armoury.

ⓐ Al-Ayubi Road ❶ 6 568 3444 Ⓦ www.shjmuseum.gov.ae/museums/islamic ◐ 09.00–13.00 & 17.00–20.00 Sat, Sun, Tues–Thur, 16.30–20.30 Fri, closed Mon; admission free

Natural History Museum & Desert Park

The desert landscape is not an easy habitat for flora and fauna to survive and thrive in, so this is a fascinating museum examining how the animals and plant life of the region have adapted to the conditions. Children will love the petting zoo, and those interested in conservation will be drawn to the area dedicated to breeding endangered Arabian animals.

ⓐ After the Sharjah International Airport at interchange No 8 ❶ 6 431 1411 Ⓦ www.shjmuseum.gov.ae/museums/natural ◐ 09.00–19.00 Mon–Thur & Sat, 10.00–20.00 Fri, closed Sun; admission free

Sharjah Archaeological Museum

A modern museum housing an ancient past. Among the exhibits are items that have been excavated dating back to around 7,000 years ago, when the first tribes settled on the peninsula. The history of the relics is informatively explained in both Arabic and English.

ⓐ Al-Hizam Al-Akhdar Road ❶ 6 566 5466 Ⓦ www. archaeology.

gov.ae 🕓 09.00–13.00 & 17.00–20.00 Mon–Thur & Sat, 17.00–20.00
Fri, closed Sun, women only Wed evening; admission free

Sharjah Heritage Museum

The Heritage Museum is a collection of several buildings that
have been brought together and restored in order to illustrate
Arabian life in days gone by. Among the buildings are family
homes, a souk and two forts, all furnished as they would have
been in their original time and setting.

ⓐ Al-Ayubi Road ☎ 6 569 3999 ⓦ www.shjmuseum.gov.ae/
museums/heritage 🕓 09.00–13.00 & 16.00–20.00 Sat, Sun &
Tues–Thur, 16.30–20.30 Fri, closed Mon, women & children only
Wed evening; admission free

CULTURE

In 1993 work was started in the Al-Shuwaiheyn area to build a
Centre for Fine Arts. Work was completed in 1995 and today the area
is the cultural heartland of the Emirate. It houses the head office of
the Emirates Fine Arts Society, the Arts Centre for studying art, the
Art Galleries, where local artists display their work, and the Very
Special Arts House, where disabled people are taught art. The new
Sharjah Art Museum is across the street.

Sharjah Art Museum

This state-of-the-art facility houses a permanent collection of
Islamic artists on the ground floor, and exhibits a changing
programme of both local and international artists on the

● *The mosque in Sharjah*

second floor. There is also a coffee shop, library and souvenir shop on site.

ⓐ Al-Shuwaiheyn near Al-Boorj Avenue ⓣ 6 568 8222
ⓦ www.sharjah-welcome.com ⓛ 09.00–13.00 & 17.00–20.00
Tues–Sun, closed Mon; admission free

RETAIL THERAPY

Blue Souk (Central Souk) The largest of Sharjah's shopping areas, with over 600 shops, selling everything from clothing to jewellery to electric goods. The main focus here, however, is on the carpets. Even if you can't afford to buy, be sure to visit the souk just for the atmosphere and nonstop haggling. ⓐ Al-Majaz, end of the Corniche Road, close to Khaled Lagoon ⓦ www.sharjah.org/html/sh_trainfo_blue_souk.htm ⓛ 09.00–13.00 & 16.00–23.00 Sat–Thur, 09.00–12.00 & 16.00–23.00

Sahara Center This mall features more than 150 shops, striking architecture including replica tent roofs, many open areas, as well as an indoor entertainment park, food court, several restaurants and an eight-screen multiplex cinema. ⓐ Al-Nahda interchange on the border with Dubai ⓣ 6 531 3666 ⓦ www.saharacentre.com ⓛ 10.00–22.00 Sat–Thur, 14.00–22.00 Fri

Sharjah City Center Everything you could possibly need – from designer clothes to everyday toiletries – can be found in this large mall opened in 2001. There's also an area designed to keep kids amused while the adults shop, and plenty of places to stop for a coffee or a snack. ⓐ Al-Wahda Street ⓣ 6 533 2626

TAKING A BREAK

Al-Gahwa Al-Shahbya £–££ A lovely place to stop and enjoy a
mint tea or a soft drink among the locals, while looking out
across the lagoon, dotted with reflections of the city lights.
Not far from the new mosque. ☎ 6 572 3788

Automatic Restaurant £–££ A Lebanese-style cafeteria restaurant
conveniently located on the Corniche. Try the mezze to sample a
little of a lot of dishes. ⓐ Al-Buhaira Corniche ☎ 6 574 1147

Caffe Undici £–££ A popular coffee spot with tables both inside
(air conditioned) and out. ⓐ Marbella Resort Marina, Khalid Lagoon
☎ 6 574 1111 ⓦ www.marbellaresort.com

AFTER DARK

Thriveni Restaurant £–££ A really inexpensive restaurant that serves
breakfast, lunch and dinner. The upper floor in particular is always
crowded and tables are almost uncomfortably close together, but
that's all part of the Arabic experience. ⓐ Rolla Square ☎ 6 562 6901

Clay Oven ££ The large tandoor oven at the entrance here assures
you that the tandoori chicken is both fresh and authentically made.
ⓐ Buhaira Lagoon ☎ 6 556 2312

Sadaf Al-Mina ££–£££ The décor can only be described as 'over the
top' and the service can be annoyingly attentive, but the food is
great. A favourite with local Emirati families who dine behind
screens. ⓐ Al-Mina Road ☎ 6 569 3344

ACCOMMODATION

Sharjah Youth Hostel £ Conveniently located near the centre of town, and just 500 m from the beach. Amenities include air conditioning, satellite TV, safety-deposit boxes and a dining room. ⓐ Sharjah centre Al-Sharghan ❶ 6 298 8151 ⓦ www.uaeyha.com

Al-Sharq Hotel ££ Located in the heart of the business district. Amenities include satellite TV, mini fridge, on-site restaurant with 24-hour room service and safety-deposit lockers. ⓐ Al-Rolla Square ❶ 6 562 0000 ⓦ www.sharqhotel.com

City Hotel Sharjah ££ Another central hotel with all the same facilities as the Al-Sharq. ⓐ Al-Rolla Square ❶ 6 561 5600

Sadaf Furnished Suites ££–£££ Sadaf offers a range of fully furnished suites from small to large, depending on your needs and the number of people you are travelling with. ⓐ Al-Mina Road ❶ 6 568 6111 ⓦ www.sadaff.com

Hotel Holiday International £££ Features cosy balconies that overlook Khalid Lagoon. The hotel has three restaurants (one open 24 hours), swimming pool, sauna, steam room, Jacuzzi and tennis courts. It's a particularly good choice if you're travelling with children, as there's an on-site playground and a separate children's pool. ⓐ Khalid Lagoon ❶ 6 573 6666 ⓦ www.holidayinternational.com

Sharjah Plaza Hotel £££ This is an apartment hotel that is located in the heart of the business centre of Sharjah and is a good option if you want a little more independence than a hotel offers. Amenities include air conditioning, television, mini fridge and an on-site restaurant providing 24-hour room service. ⓐ PO Box 1281, Sharjah ⓣ 6 561 7000

Sharjah Rotana Hotel £££ Sharjah Rotana is a luxury hotel that features fully equipped rooms, a fitness centre, steam rooms, an outdoor swimming pool, three restaurants/bars and access to an exclusive beach club. ⓐ Al-Arouba Street ⓣ 6 563 7777 ⓦ www.sharjahrotana.com

Marbella Resort £££ This luxury resort is nestled on Khalid Lagoon and has 50 individual fully equipped villas of various sizes. On-site amenities include two swimming pools, tennis courts, air-conditioned squash courts, gymnasium, sauna, steam bath and several restaurants and shops. ⓐ Khalid Lagoon ⓣ 6 574 1111 ⓦ www.marbellaresort.com

Millennium Hotel £££ Overlooking Khalid Lagoon, this super-luxurious hotel features several restaurants, three swimming pools, a full health club and a squash court. ⓐ Corniche Road ⓣ 6 556 6666 ⓦ www.millenniumhotels.com

Fujairah

Fujairah is one of the most physically beautiful areas of the UAE, although it has only very recently begun to attract tourists. The coastline stretches for some 90 km (56 miles) along the Gulf of Oman and the interior is known for its colourful rugged mountains and spectacular waterfalls. In addition this ancient area has a number of sites that will be of interest to archaeology buffs, and ancient ruins of forts and mosques.

Its main attraction for tourists, however, is the opportunity it offers for extreme and water sports. Paragliding, wind surfing,

● *Into the fray: bull-fighting is a popular sport*

water-skiing and jet-skiing have all become popular in this ocean-side resort. And the beaches are among the best in the Emirates.

GETTING THERE

Fujairah is about 130 km (80 miles) east of Dubai. You can hire a car in Dubai or take the minibus from Deira station, which costs Dh 25.

SIGHTS & ATTRACTIONS

Ain Al-Madhab Gardens

When the summer temperatures soar, this is a popular getaway in the foothills of the Hajar Mountains. Natural rock pools and springs are the perfect way to cool off, and there are facilities for both men and women in the traditional Islamic way.

🕐 10.00–23.00 Sun–Fri, closed Sat

Bull-fighting

A major attraction in Fujairah is the opportunity to view the Emirate's own unique style of bull-fighting. Don't expect any flash matadors though – this is a fight between bull and bull: they lock horns and wrestle until the weaker of the two gives up and turns away. It may seem a pointless exercise, and there's no gore for those expecting blood spillage, but it's very popular among the locals.

ⓐ Near the Al-Rughlait Bridge 🕐 16.30 Fri

Fujairah Heritage Village

Another museum dedicated to Arabian life in days gone by. Traditional houses, cooking utensils, farm tools and other items all help explain life in the desert through the ages.

🅐 Close to the Ain Al-Madhab Gardens 🕐 10.00–23.00 Sun–Fri, closed Sat

Fujairah Museum
Located in the former home of Sheikh Zayed, the museum is dedicated to the history of the region, with excavated archaeological finds, and ancient jewellery and weapons on display.
🅘 9 222 9085 🕐 08.00–13.00 & 16.00–18.00 Sun–Fri, closed Sat; admission charge

ACCOMMODATION

Fujairah Beach Motel £££ Despite its name, this hotel is not on the beach, so don't expect to walk straight on to sand as you leave your room. The rooms are also quite basic and most have twin beds. The hotel has a restaurant and a choice of three bars (Arabic, Indian and Pakistani). 🅘 9 222 8111

Ritz Plaza Hotel ££ Clean and efficient accommodation, although applying the word 'Ritz' to its name is definitely a case of having ideas above its station. 🅐 Hamad Bin Abdullah Street 🅘 9 222 2202

Al-Diar Siji Hotel £££ One of the more recent additions to Fujairah, the hotel is aimed at a business clientele, which may explain its somewhat soulless ambiance. Rooms are of the 4-star variety, and there are tennis courts, a bowling alley, gym and restaurant available. 🅐 Al-Sharqui Road 🅘 9 223 2000
🅦 www.aldiarhotels.com/siji-hotel.html

◀ *Fruit aplenty at Fujairah market*

Fujairah Hilton £££ The Hilton is one of the best options in the area. All rooms have a view of the sea and there are separate chalets for family groups. ⓐ Al-Ghourfa Road ⓣ 9 222 2411 ⓦ www.hiltonworldresorts.com/resorts/Fujairah/index.html

RETAIL THERAPY

Masafi Friday Market Despite its name, the Masafi Market operates every day. Situated on the road between the Hajar Mountains and Fujairah City, it's the best place to come for traditional wares and pottery made from Fujairah clay.

TAKING A BREAK

Maharath Al-Bahar Cafeteria & Restaurant £ Eat in or take away. This restaurant serves up fresh sandwiches and freshly squeezed fruit juices and is a local favourite. Open for breakfast, lunch and dinner. ⓐ Hamad bin Abdullah Road ⓣ 9 222 6963 ⓛ 08.00–23.00

AFTER DARK

Taj Mahal £ The Taj Mahal is true to its name, featuring Indian dishes and a particularly good choice for vegetarians. The service is surprisingly good for such a low-budget venue. For dessert you can actually indulge in Häagen-Dazs ice cream. ⓐ Hamad Bin Sultan Road ⓣ 9 222 5225

Neptunia Restaurant ££ A pleasant poolside restaurant with views of the Indian Ocean. À la carte or buffet choices reflect both local and Indian cuisine – and there's a good wine list. ⓐ Furjairah Hilton, Al-Ghourfa Road ⓣ 9 222 2411 ⓦ www.hilton.com

Tropicana ££ A fun and funky nightspot with live entertainment every evening. The clientele is mostly businessmen.
ⓐ Furjairah Hilton, Al-Ghourfa Road ⓣ 9 222 2411
ⓦ www.hilton.com/en/hi/hotels/dining.jhtml?ctyhocn=SHJHITW

⬥ *Fujairah Old Fort*

OUT OF TOWN

Muscat, Oman

Muscat, the capital of Oman, seems to be on the fast track to becoming the next hot tourist destination on the Arabian Peninsula. If you want to dally in an area with more palm trees than high-rise buildings, Muscat is the place to visit. Muscat is the umbrella name for the many small municipalities that are strung along the coast of Oman, each covering a land area of little more than 3 or 4 km (1¾–2½ miles), including Muttruh and Ruwi.

In ancient times, Muscat was a thriving and strategically important port of the Arabian Peninsula. Today its appearance is both modern and medieval, with new buildings juxtaposed with two old Portuguese forts. Not so dazzling or futuristic as Dubai, Muscat and its environs give more of a taste of the everyday and normal life in the Gulf. Just outside the city area you'll discover a wide range of landscapes, from serene beaches to rugged mountains and intimidating deserts.

GETTING THERE

It's about 380 km (236 miles) from Dubai to Muscat and there are regular flights between the two cities. Hiring a car is another option, but you need separate insurance to cover you in Oman. There is a twice-daily minibus service to Muscat run by Dubai Transport, which takes around six hours; or you can engage a long-distance taxi, but you must fill all the seats or pay for them all; ensure you fix the price beforehand. A tax is payable when crossing the border.

GETTING AROUND

Once in Oman, and if you haven't got a car, taxis are the best way to see the region, but be sure to negotiate the fare first. Taxis may be arranged for one-way trips, by the hour or by the day. To keep your transport costs down, look for the service taxis, which can carry up to five passengers and follow set routes. Bus trips can be somewhat difficult and should be avoided by women travelling alone. It is possible to rent both a car and a driver, usually from a hotel. If you plan to explore the outer regions of the area, a 4WD vehicle is your best choice.

LOCAL ETIQUETTE

As in most Islamic regions, the visitor is wise to err on the side of conservatism. Do not point directly at people, never allow people to see the soles of your feet or shoes and do not kiss, hug or hold hands in public. It is considered impolite to smoke in public. Alcohol is not strictly illegal but be sure to consume it only in licensed establishments. And, don't forget when taking photographs to be sure to ask permission first; avoid taking photographs of women or military establishments altogether.

SIGHTS & ATTRACTIONS

Grand Mosque

This modern and quietly imposing structure was a gift to the nation of Oman from Sultan Qaboos to mark the 30th year of his reign in 2001. The carpet inside is said to be the largest in the world and purportedly took 600 women four years to weave. Non-Muslims are allowed to visit during specific hours. Be sure to

wear long sleeves, a long skirt or trousers (not jeans), and women
should cover their hair.
ⓐ Sultan Qaboos Street ⓒ 08.00–11.00 Sat–Wed, closed Thur & Fri

Marina Bandar Al-Rowdha

If you're into water sports, head to the marina, where there are jet
skis on hire. This is also the boarding point for dolphin cruises along
the Gulf Coast. If you're an avid sea fisherman, you can charter boats
here too.
ⓐ Central Muscat ⓣ 968 24 737 288

Marine Science & Fisheries Centre

An excellent choice for anyone interested in marine life, particularly
the wealth of fish and sea life along the Gulf Coast.
ⓐ Between the Al-Bustan Palace Hotel and the Capital Area Yacht
Club, Muscat ⓣ 968 24 740 061

Natural History Museum

Everything from a whale skeleton to shells, as well as plants and
displays about the environment, await the visitor here. A good place
to learn a lot about the local habitat.
ⓐ Housed within the Ministry of National Heritage & Culture,
Muscat ⓣ 968 24 605 400 ⓒ 09.00–13.00 & 16.00–18.00 Sat–Thur,
16.00–18.00 Fri

Old Muttrah Souk

The charming chaos of this cavernous marketplace is a classic
example of the traditional souk. Everything from gold and silver to

---

ⓓ *Al-Bustan InterContinental Palace Hotel*

spices, gaudy Arabian materials, household goods and souvenirs await your bargaining skills.

ⓐ Located along the Muttrah Cornice, Muscat

Oman Museum

Everything you could want to know about Oman's 5,000 year history is uncovered here, with particularly good exhibits dedicated to local architecture and shipbuilding, which has played an important role in the region.

ⓐ Ministries Area in Medinat Qaboos, Muscat ☎ 968 24 600 946
🕐 09.00–13.00 & 16.00–18.00 Sat–Thur, 16.00–18.00 Fri

Sultan's Armed Forces Museum

Weapons and armoury are the order of the day here, as the museum uncovers Oman's military history from pre-Islamic times to the present day.

ⓐ Located in Ruwi, Bait Al-Falaj – behind the Muscat Municipality, Muscat ☎ 968 24 312 648 🕐 08.00–13.30 Sun, Mon, Wed & Thur, closed Tues, Fri & Sat

RETAIL THERAPY

Al-Araimi Centre Al-Araimi is a popular meeting place and great find for the latest in European and International fashion and accessories. Home to well-known brand names such as JCPenney, Giordano, Mexx, as well as luxury designer goods from Rolex and Versace. Also houses shops dealing in music, electronics, perfumes, sports gear and furniture. Plenty of fast-food outlets for when all that shopping

◀ *Idyllic beaches are a big attraction*

affects your appetite.  Located in the Qurum Area shopping district, Muscat ☏ 968 24 566 180
🌐 www.muscatmall.com/alaraimi.htm

Al-Khamis Plaza Also in the Qurum shopping district, Al-Khamis Plaza is a bustling shopping centre of trendy fashion boutiques, exclusive fashion jewellery and designer stores. The plaza also features music and computer stores and a coffee shop.
📍 Located in the Qurum area shopping district, Muscat
☏ 968 24 563 009

TAKING A BREAK

Internet cafés
Cyberworld £ This large Internet café also provides a huge range of snacks – pizzas, quiches, sandwiches, drinks and more.
📍 Alasfoor Plaza, Qurum Commercial Area ☏ 968 24 566 740
🕐 09.00–13.00 & 16.30–20.30 Sat–Thur, closed Fri

New Millenium Generation Trading £ Broadband provision, printing and refreshments in a welcoming environment. 📍 Next to National Bank of Oman, Corniche, Muttrah, Muscat ☏ 99 562 708
🕐 09.00–01.00

AFTER DARK

Restaurants
Blue Cactus ££ Really good Western food, cocktails and a natural setting. 📍 Located at the top of Qurum Natural Park
☏ 968 24 605 255

Tuscany ££–£££ Exceptionally good Italian food accompanied by top-notch service. ⓐ Grand Hyatt Muscat, Shatti Al-Qurum
ⓣ 968 24 641 234

Mumtaz Mahal £££ Possibly the best Indian food in Oman, but also the most expensive. However, the view makes it worth parting with the extra money. ⓐ Located at the top of Qurum Natural Park
ⓣ 968 24 605 907

ACCOMMODATION

Dream Resort £ Clean, quiet and somewhat spartan. ⓐ Dama Street
ⓣ 968 24 453 399

Majan Continental Hotel £ Largely catering to a business clientele, this is a pleasant accommodation option, with pool, health centre – and even a British-style pub, complete with dartboard and billiards table. ⓐ Al-Burj Street ⓣ 968 24 592 900
ⓦ www.majanhotel.com

Ramada Qurum Beach Hotel £ Everything you'd expect from a chain hotel including satellite TV, conference facilities and an excellent buffet breakfast. ⓐ Sarooj Street ⓣ 968 24 603 555
ⓦ www.ramada.com

Crowne Plaza Hotel ££ Set on a cliff top in the suburb of Qurum, the hotel commands one of the most photographed views in the region. The amenities include all you might expect from a 4-star hotel. ⓐ Bldg 1730, Qurum Street ⓣ 968 24 660 660
ⓦ www.ichotelsgroup.com

Al-Bustan InterContinental Palace Hotel £££ Originally constructed as a meeting place for the Arabian Gulf Co-Operation Council heads of state, it is one of the most luxurious hotels in this part of the world. Internet connections, swimming pools and squash and tennis courts are just a few of the amenities available. ⓐ On the beachfront off the Al Sultan Qaboos dual carriageway, 10 minutes from the financial district of Ruwi (it is clearly signposted) ⓣ 968 24 799 666 ⓦ www.al-bustan.intercontinental.com

Grand Hyatt Muscat £££ One of the loveliest resorts in the Gulf, the Grand Hyatt Resort is spread over 4 hectares (10 acres) of soft, sandy beaches in the Shatti Al-Qurm area. Restaurants, nightclubs, lounges and plenty of sport facilities. ⓐ Shatti Al-Qurm ⓣ 968 24 641 234 ⓦ www.muscat.grand.hyatt.com

---

ⓓ *UAE dirhams*

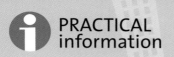

PRACTICAL information

Directory

GETTING THERE

Dubai's location at the crossroads of Europe and Asia makes it easily accessible from anywhere in Europe, the Middle East and almost everywhere else. Options for travelling to Dubai include air, bus, car and ship. There are no rail routes leading to Dubai.

The national airline is government-owned Emirates, which flies to over 80 destinations in the Middle East, Europe, Australia, Africa, Asia, the Indian subcontinent and the USA. In fact, Dubai is a popular refuelling point for long-haul flights, so it makes the perfect stopover point if travelling from Europe to Asia or Australia. As an added bonus the duty-free shop at Dubai airport is one of the largest in the world.

By air

From the UK and Europe All the major European capitals, as well as other major cities in larger countries, have direct flights to Dubai on various airlines (see page 56).

From North America Emirates has recently inaugurated a nonstop service from New York to Dubai. From other destinations in North America you will need to change flights, most likely in London, Paris or Zurich.

Many people are aware that air travel emits CO_2, which contributes to climate change. You may be interested in the possibility of lessening the environmental impact of your flight through the charity Climate Care, which offsets your CO_2 by funding environmental projects around the world. Visit Ⓦ www.climatecare.org

By bus

It is possible, if not always comfortable, to travel around most parts of the UAE by bus. The Dubai Transport minibus service operates between Dubai and Muscat in Oman, Egypt and Jordan – contact a local travel agent for times of departures. In Dubai itself the main bus route is between Hatta and Deira.

By taxi

Long-distance taxis are a good option if you are travelling in a party of more than two people – otherwise it's an expensive choice, as you usually have to pay for all five seats even if they're not occupied. You will also have to pay a border-crossing tax if travelling from countries outside the UAE.

By ferry

Water travel is always a romantic way to arrive at any destination, but in Dubai it does mean travelling to and from the troubled regions of Iran and Iraq, which is currently inadvisable.

ENTRY FORMALITIES

Visa requirements

British nationals do not need a visa to enter the UAE and can stay in the region for one month providing they have a valid passport. If you require a longer stay, you can apply for a visa for a three-month sojourn and repeat as necessary.

Visitors from the USA, Canada, Australia, New Zealand and most Western European and Far Eastern countries are entitled to a free extendable visit visa on arrival.

Another popular option is to apply for a hotel visa. This means that the hotel that you are staying in sponsors your visit, with either a 15-day transit visa or a 30-day visit visa. If you want to stay for more than a fortnight, opt for the latter – transit visas cannot be extended.

⬤ *The ferry terminal in Dubai*

Customs

On entering Dubai, foreign visitors may bring with them up to 2,000 cigarettes, 400 cigars or 2 kg of loose tobacco, providing it is for personal use. Non-Muslims are permitted to import 2 litres of wine and 2 litres of spirits. However, if you are entering Dubai from Sharjah, where alcohol is prohibited, you will not be able to bring any with you into Dubai.

Personal belongings are exempt from duties, but if videos or DVDs are among your possessions, expect them to be screened – customs officials have a list of banned films and other materials that are considered unacceptable by the Islamic faith or that might incite Muslims to convert to another religion.

MONEY

The monetary unit is the dirham (Dh) which is divided into 100 fils.

Bank opening hours are 08.00–13.00 Saturday to Wednesday, although some also open 16.30–18.30. On Thursdays, banks close at 12.00: remember Thursday and Friday form the weekend in Dubai. Bureaux de change are generally open 08.30–13.00 and 16.30–20.30.

HEALTH, SAFETY & CRIME

The Middle East has long had its political problems, making many areas no-go for tourists, but on the whole, Dubai and the rest of the UAE are relatively trouble free. It's always advisable, however, to check your own country's foreign-office advice prior to travel.

There is a very low crime rate in this area due to a number of factors: the strict Islamic code of behaviour, rigorously enforced laws and a low unemployment rate. The exception to safety in Dubai and the UAE is the dangerous behaviour of those behind

the wheel of a car. Out on the road is where you need to be your most cautious.

OPENING HOURS

Most businesses are open 08.00–13.00 and 16.00–19.00 Saturday to Wednesday. Thursday afternoon and Friday is the weekend in the Islamic world. Many companies may therefore close at 13.00 on Thursday afternoon.

TOILETS

In Dubai it is always best to use the facilities when you have an opportunity. Public toilets are almost nonexistent. However, the major hotels and shopping centres have plenty that are Western-style and well maintained. When venturing away from the city, be prepared for the more primitive squat-style facilities.

CHILDREN

Emiratis love children and are inclined to spoil them during the day. However, unless there are special activities taking place, you will rarely see children out in the evenings. Hotels are generally accommodating and can provide cots or even a crib with advance notice. Special infant needs such as nappies and baby food can be readily found in the hypermarkets of the malls, and in addition most of the shopping centres provide a children's play area.

Dubai has plenty of child-friendly sights and activities on offer. From the amusement centres of the Breakwater in Abu Dhabi to the water parks such as Wild Wadi (see page 110), to more cultural attractions such as the Dubai Zoo (see page 102) and the Heritage Village (see page 84), you won't have any difficulty finding ways to keep your young traveller amused.

CUSTOMS, RELIGION & ETIQUETTE

Language

The official language is Arabic but English is both widely spoken and understood, as are Farsi, Hindi and Urdu. Both Arabic and English are commonly used in business and commerce.

Religion

Islam is the official religion of the UAE and there are a large number of mosques throughout the city. While other religions are freely tolerated, visitors are expected to abide by the Islamic code of conduct. Dubai has a small number of Christian churches, Protestant, Roman Catholic and Greek Orthodox, as well as both Shiva and Krishna temples

Ramadan

Ramadan is the holy month in which Muslims commemorate the revelation of the Holy Koran. The timing of Ramadan is not fixed in terms of the Western calendar but according to the lunar calendar, which means its exact dates each year may not be decided until a few days in advance. It is a month of fasting when Muslims abstain from food, drinks and cigarettes from sunrise to sunset.

❶ Visitors are also required to refrain from consuming these items in public places during this time as a sign of respect.

Alcohol

Alcohol is available in hotel and club restaurants and bars. However, restaurants outside the hotels are not permitted to serve alcoholic beverages. Permanent residents who are non-Muslims can obtain liquor supplies without difficulty under a permit system.

Photography

If you're just taking general tourist snapshots, photography is no problem, although it is always courteous to ask permission when photographing people, and taking shots of Muslim women should be avoided. Do not take photographs of any government or military buildings – if caught you are likely to be questioned and have your film (or digital camera) confiscated.

COMMUNICATIONS

Phone

To call the UAE from abroad, the country code is 971 followed by the city code and the local number. Communications are excellent in Dubai. Telephones have international direct dialling to most countries.

Your UK, New Zealand and Australian mobile phone will work in Dubai; US and Canadian cellphones will not. Travellers from those countries can solve this easily with a universal mobile from Mobal, a UK firm with cutting-edge expertise in international communications. These mobiles will work anywhere in the world with a permanent UK number that travels with you (UK ☏ 1 543 426 999 ✆ 1 543 426 126 🌐 www.mobell.co.uk; US ☏ 888 888 9162 (free call) or 212 785 58 00 🌐 www.mobalrental.com

Post

Dubai can boast an efficient and reliable postal service. The General Postal Authority also offers a courier service, Mumtaz Post, which delivers to most parts of the world. Commercial courier services are also widely used.

Central Post Office ⓐ Zabeel Road, Karama ⓣ 4 337 1500
ⓛ 08.00–23.30 Sat–Wed, 16.00–20.00 Fri

Deira Post Office ⓐ Al-Sabkha Road, near the intersection of
Baniyas ⓛ 08.00–24.00 Sat–Wed, 08.00–13.00 & 16.00–20.00 Thur,
closed Fri

Internet

This is one of the most electronically savvy cities in the world. Most
accommodation, even hostels, has some kind of email or internet
service available.

City Bowling Internet ⓐ Deira City Centre ⓣ 4 295 9139
ⓛ 10.00–02.00; around Dh 15 per hour

Golden Fork ⓐ Al-Maktoum Road, Deira ⓣ 4 228 2662
ⓛ 10.00–04.00; around Dh 5 per hour

Newspapers and television

There are two English-language newspapers published in Dubai –
the *Gulf News* and *Khaleej Times*. International newspapers,
magazines and journals can be readily purchased in bookshops
and supermarkets.

Dubai has both Arabic and English commercial radio and television
stations, as well as access to international satellite programming.

ELECTRICITY

The electricity supply in Dubai is 220/240 volts at 50 cycles. British
electronic goods will need a plug adapter; US-made appliances will
need a transformer.

DRESS CODE

Dubai has a subtropical, arid climate. You can expect clear blue skies and very little rain most of the year, so summer clothing should be packed even if the temperature at home is near freezing. From November to April, however, remember to include a lightweight sweater or jacket – the desert temperature can drop surprisingly quickly after sunset.

Despite its Islamic faith, the dress code in Dubai is relatively relaxed – swimsuits, bikinis and swimming trunks will not be frowned upon if you're sunbathing by the pool or on the beach. However, when walking the streets and visiting tourist attractions it is expected to show some conservatism, covering upper arms, cleavage and thighs. Men should not walk around bare-chested. In Oman, women should avoid short skirts or dresses; tightly fitting clothes and brief shorts are also unacceptable. Swimwear should only ever be worn by the pool or on the beach.

WATER

Tap water is quite safe to drink but not very palatable. Bottled mineral water is on sale everywhere.

TRAVELLERS WITH DISABILITIES

Dubai, for all its modern façade, still lags behind in amenities for the disabled. All the major shopping centres have wheelchair access, but ramps in car parks and into most buildings are few. The Dubai Museum has ramps but other tourist attractions may prove difficult, if not impossible, to navigate. Dubai airport is well equipped and even has low check-in counters. Although many hotels claim to have good wheelchair access, be sure to check first. www.dubaitourism.ae lists accessible sites, cinemas and shopping centres. If you need more information, RADAR is a company that offers advice for disabled travellers around the world.

ⓐ 12 City Forum, 250 City Road, London EC1V 8AF, UK

ⓣ 020 7250 3222 ⓦ www.radar.org.uk

TOURIST INFORMATION
Tourist Offices – Dubai
Department of Tourism & Commerce Marketing (DTCM) Welcome Bureau

The DTCM operates a number of bureaux scattered throughout the city where you'll generally find maps, details of sights and their opening hours and exhibitions, and bus schedules.

ⓐ Beni Yas Square, Deira ⓣ 4 228 5000 ⓕ 4 228 0011
ⓦ www.dubaitourism.co.ae ⓛ 09.00-21.00 Sat–Thur, 15.00–21.00 Fri

Dubai National Tourist & Transport Authority

This large and well-run government tourist agency can assist you with transport and accommodation throughout the UAE.

ⓐ Al-Maktoum Road, Deira ⓣ 4 295 1111 ⓛ 09.00–18.00 Sat–Thur, closed Fri

Useful Websites

ⓦ www.dubaitourism.co.ae

ⓦ www.godubai.com

ⓦ www.uae-pages.com/tourism

ⓦ www.uae.org.ae

ⓦ www.dubaicityguide.com

Useful phrases

Dubai's official language is Arabic, though English is widely spoken and understood. Arabic is a tricky language for English-speakers to learn – the beautiful script is particularly difficult to master. Don't panic! You'll get by perfectly well in Dubai with English but if you fancy trying out a bit of Arabic, here are some useful words and phrases with an approximate English pronunciation.

English	*Approx. pronunciation*
BASICS	
Yes	*naahm*
No	*laa*
OK	*hasanan*
Please	*min fadlak*
Thank you (very much)	*shukran (jazeelan)*
Sorry	*aasif*
Excuse me (to get attention)	*lau samaht*
Pardon?	*ahfwan?*
My name is ...	*ismee ...*
Hello	*marhaban*
Hi	*ahlan*
Good morning	*sabaah al-khayr*
Good afternoon/evening	*masaa al-khayr*
Good night	*tisbah ahla khayr*
I'm lost	*ana tuht*
Where is/are ...?	*ayn ...?*
Can you show me where I am on the map?	*mumkin tareenee ayn ana ahlaal khareeta?*
Where are the toilets?	*ayn al-hammaamaat?*
Thanks for your help	*shukran ahlaal musaahda*
Do you speak English?	*tatkallam injileezee?*
I don't speak much Arabic	*laa atkallam ahrabee kateer*
I understand	*afham*
I don't understand	*laa afham*
Do you accept traveller's cheques?	*hal taqbal sheekaat siyaaheeya?*
I'll pay ...	*sa-adfah ...*
by cash	*naqdan*
by credit card	*bi-bitaaqat itimaan*

English	*Approx. pronunciation*

SHOPPING

English	*Approx. pronunciation*
How much is it?	*bikam haaza?*
Can you write it down, please?	*hal mumkin taktubuh, lau samaht?*
That's too expensive	*haaza ghaalee jiddan*
I'll take it	*sa-aakhuduh*
Can I try this on?	*hal astateeah an ujarrib haaza?*
It doesn't fit	*laa yulaa'imnee*
It fits well. I'll take it	*innuh yulaa'imnee jiddan. sa-aakhuduh*

EATING OUT

Breakfast	*al-futoor*
Lunch	*al-ghada*
Dinner	*al-ahsha*
Waiter/Waitress	*yaa garsoon/yaa aanisa*
I'd like ...	*ureed ...*
Do you have a set menu?	*hal ladaykum tabaq al-yaum*
Do you have vegetarian meals?	*ahndak wajbaat lin-nabaatiyeen*
The bill please	*al-hisaab, lau samaht*

EMERGENCIES

Help!	*an-najda!*
Go away!	*insarif/imshee!*
Stop thief!	*imsik haraamee!*
Fire!	*hareeq!*
Call the police!	*ittasil bish-shurta!*
Call a doctor!	*ittasil bi-duktoor!*

NUMBERS

One	*waahid*	Nine	*tisaha*
Two	*itnayn*	Ten	*ahshara*
Three	*talaata*	Eleven	*hadashar*
Four	*arbaha*	Twelve	*itnashar*
Five	*khamsa*	Twenty	*ahishreen*
Six	*sitta*	Fifty	*khamseen*
Seven	*sabaha*	One hundred	*mi'a*
Eight	*tamaanya*		

Emergencies

Fire 997
Ambulance 998
Police 999

POLICE

In general the Dubai police are most helpful. You will even find 'Tourist Police' in the souks and other attractions to help with language difficulties and directions. Any crime, large or small, should be reported to the police immediately, including any car accidents.

MEDICAL

Medical facilities in Dubai are of an international standard. However, to avoid high costs should you require medical treatment make sure you have comprehensive travel insurance before leaving home.

Dubai Hospital This facility operates a 24-hour emergency department. ⓐ Abu Baker Al-Siddiq Road near the corner of Al-Khaleej Road, Hor al-Anz ⓣ 4 271 4444

Dubai London Clinic A private medical centre that operates an emergency facility. ⓐ Al-Wasi Road, Jumeirah ⓣ 4 344 6663

CONSULATES & EMBASSIES

British Embassy
🖿 Al-Seef Street
☎ 4 309 4444

Australian Consulate General
🖿 Emarat Atrium, Sheikh Zayed Road, Dubai
☎ 4 321 2444

Canadian Consulate General
🖿 United Bank Building, Khaleed bin Al-Waleed Street
☎ 4 352 1717

South African Embassy
🖿 Sharaf Building, 3rd Floor, Khaleed bin Al-Waleed Street
☎ 4 397 5222

United States Embassy
🖿 21st Floor, World Trade Centre
☎ 4 311 6000

The publishers would like to thank the following individuals and organisations for supplying copyright photographs for this book:
Christopher Holt: all images except:
Brian McMorrow pages 7, 12, 21, 22, 30, 33, 41
Pictures Colour Library: pages 5, 137, 138

Copy editor: Penny Isaac
Proofreader: Emma Sangster

Send your thoughts to
books@thomascook.com

- **Found a great bar, club, shop or must-see sight that we don't feature?**

- **Like to tip us off about any information that needs updating?**

- **Want to tell us what you love about this handy little guidebook and more importantly how we can make it even handier?**

Then here's your chance to tell all! Send us ideas, discoveries and recommendations today and then look out for your valuable input in the next edition of this title. As an extra 'thank you' from Thomas Cook Publishing, you'll be automatically entered into our exciting monthly prize draw.

Send an email to the above address (stating the book's title) or write to: CitySpots Project Editor, Thomas Cook Publishing, PO Box 227, The Thomas Cook Business Park, Unit 18, Coningsby Road, Peterborough PE3 8SB, UK.